Hybrids of Modernity

Hybrids of Modernity considers the relationship between three western modernist institutions: anthropology, the nation state and the universal exhibition. It looks at the ways in which these institutions are linked, how they are engaged in the objectification of culture, and how they have themselves become objects of cultural theory – the target of critics who claim that despite their continuing visibility these are all institutions with questionable viability in the late twentieth century.

How and to what effect are representational and practice approaches brought together in the self-conscious production of culture? And what of the relationship between anthropology and cultural studies, between theory and ethnography, between representational knowledge and knowledge as embodied practice?

Through an analysis of the Universal Exhibition held in Seville in 1992, the themes of culture, nationality and technology are explored. *Hybrids of Modernity* pays particular attention to how 'culture' is produced and put to work by the national and corporate participants, and to the relationship between the emergence of culture as a commodity and the way in which the concept is employed in contemporary cultural theory.

Penelope Harvey is Senior Lecturer in Social Anthropology, University of Manchester.

Hybrids of Modernity

Anthropology, the nation state and the universal exhibition

Penelope Harvey

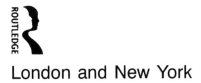

London and New York

First published 1996
by Routledge
11 New Fetter Lane, London EC4P 4EE

Simultaneously published in the USA and Canada
by Routledge
29 West 35th Street, New York, NY 10001

Routledge is an International Thomson Publishing company

© 1996 Penelope Harvey

Phototypeset in Times by Intype London Ltd
Printed and bound in Great Britain by
Biddles Ltd, Guildford and King's Lynn

British Library Cataloguing in Publication Data
A catalogue record for this book is available from the British Library

Library of Congress Cataloguing in Publication Data
A catalogue record for this book has been requested

ISBN 0–415–13044–1 (hbk)
ISBN 0–415–13045–X (pbk)

Contents

Figures

Acknowledgements

The research on which this book is based was a process which at times was far less planned than the end result might suggest. Along the way there were many people who helped me in those aspects of the project which I had foreseen. Others gave me ideas which radically altered its nature and helped to shape the work that has emerged. My working life in the Department of Social Anthropology at the University of Manchester, by which I mean the relationships of teaching and research, and the fights and alliances between colleagues over what matters in contemporary anthropology, provided the context and also the background support that I have drawn on to carry the project through.

It was Laura Rival who first suggested that we go together to study Expo'92 in Seville. As Americanists we were interested in the ways in which the fifth centenary of the much disputed 'discovery' of the Americas was to be marked in this European setting. Our research was funded by the British Academy but even by the time we began the fieldwork the project had shifted from our original proposal to write an ethnography of the exhibition. Nevertheless I had by then decided to write about the exhibition in a rather different frame and began to try out the ideas at various seminars. I am very grateful to all the participants who on those occasions gave me so many constructive comments. The first tentative paper was given to the seminar of the International Centre of Contemporary Cultural Research at the Universities of Manchester and Keele and I have subsequently spoken at the Centre for Cultural Values at Lancaster; the Departments of Anthropology at University College London, Swansea and Cambridge; at the Department of Anthropology in Santa Cruz, California where I also had the opportunity to discuss some of my ideas with the graduate seminar; at the Latin American Faculty of Social Sciences (FLASCO) in Quito, Ecuador and at a conference on Andean History and Anthropology hosted by the University of Jujuy, Argentina and the Bartolome de las Casas Centre for Rural Studies, Peru.

Closer to home it is the many conversations and ideas from friends and colleagues which have helped me to carry the project forward. Conversations with Jimmy Weiner, Sharon Macdonald, Kay Richardson, John Hutnyk and Jean Lave were particularly important to me. Sarah Franklin and Marilyn Strathern have both provided much of the inspiration and motivation to keep writing. Jeanette Edwards and Celia Lury gave me the impetus to finish by taking the time to read the final draft. Their support has helped me to let go of a book that I could have gone on writing for many more years!

In Spain I am grateful to Margaret Bullen, to Antonio Acosta and to Pedro Vera for their hospitality, their friendship and their interest. At home it was my parents, my oldest friend Alison Barclay and my partner Ben Campbell who helped me find the space to write and kept things going while I did. The book is dedicated to the concept of maternity leave and to Laurie for providing the sense of urgency.

Chapter 1

Introduction

THE WORLD AS EXHIBITION

Mitchell opens his book on 'the peculiar methods of order that characterize the modern West'[1] with a reminder of the nature of a peculiarity prevalent in nineteenth century Europe:

> Middle Eastern visitors found Europeans a curious people, with an uncontainable eagerness to stand and stare. 'One of the characteristics of the French is to stare and get excited at everything new', wrote an Egyptian scholar who spent five years in Paris in the 1820s. It was perhaps this staring he had in mind when he explained in another book, discussing the manners and customs of various nations, that 'one of the beliefs of the Europeans is that the gaze has no effect'.
>
> (Mitchell 1988: 2)

Today it is the turn of anthropologists to remark on this continuing European habit and to urge cultural theorists to consider the effects of such practice on both their actions and their theory. In a recent article on the temporality of the landscape, Ingold presents a painting by Bruegel, *The Harvesters*, to illustrate the difference between the landscape as picture, and the landscape in which people dwell:

> The landscape is not a totality that you or anyone else can look *at*, it is rather the world *in* which we stand in taking up a point of view on our surroundings. And it is within the context of this attentive involvement in the landscape that the human imagination gets to work in fashioning ideas about it.
>
> (Ingold 1993: 171)

Ingold invited his readers to 'imagine yourself set down in the very landscape depicted [by Bruegel], on a sultry August day in 1565. Standing a little way off to the right of the group beneath the tree, you are a witness to the scene unfolding about you' (Ingold 1993b: 165). As I tried to imagine, another scene kept coming to mind, transposing the sultry August day in 1565 on to a sweltering day in August 1992 and I began to wonder what western cultural theory would lose if it were to discard the world as picture. What if our landscape were a universal exhibition rather than Bruegel's rural scene? Or to put it another way, what happens to phenomenology when people live their world as picture? And how does this way of dwelling in the world co-exist with other ways of dwelling?

Imagine, for example, that you are witness to a scene in the Andalusian countryside. A couple sit under a tree on the edge of an olive grove. But this couple are not resting from their work as peasants, they are waiting for the bus, which arrives and carries them over the new bridge to the Island of La Cartuja, where they queue to enter the Expo'92. There they are faced with the last universal exhibition of the twentieth century,[2] an environment that has emerged through the activities of human beings with each other and with this arid island (Figure 1). The couple enter via the Triana gate and come across a strange structure, a façade where they had expected to find the Pavilion of Discovery. They remember reading that it had burnt down shortly before the exhibition was due to open, and that the exhibition space had become the venue for a discotheque. They head for the Pavilion of Navigation about which they have heard so much, but the queue is very long and they cannot imagine that they will get to the front before closing time, so they go instead to the Pavilion of Promise, and listen to the message of the American Evangelists. They queue to see Monaco's aquarium, the Fujitsu three-dimensional movie and the art treasures of the Holy See. Exhausted they sit through the sound and light show in the Czech pavilion three times, relieved to be out of the sun. And so the tour continues, as they engage with the pavilions which might become sites for the acquisition of knowledge about a nation, for the acquisition or expression of desires for consumer goods, or for the acquisition of experience which can be displayed and traded in conversations or in the form of material souvenirs, sites in which to seek shelter from the heat, places to rest weary feet, opportunities to avoid the queues. But our visitors are also aware that this environment has been carefully planned, it is the material outcome of the intentions, beliefs and values of many designers. They are interested in these plans and buy guidebooks, collect printed handouts, and talk to the hostesses and to other visitors in the queues to find out what is going on. They might engage with the reflexive ironies of the architecture, enjoy the intertextual references in some of the displays, even compare the ways in which nation states seek to present themselves. These comparisons might become the subject of their conversations, the content of their postcards home, the focus of their photographs. Or would they tell of how much they had enjoyed themselves, how they had occasionally felt bored and had returned home exhausted? Maybe. But I doubt that they returned home thinking how strange it was to see the world as exhibition.

Ingold's point on the representational model is well taken and complements Mitchell's interest in the ways in which colonial institutions (including the exhibitions) were instrumental in creating that distinction between representation and reality which came to operate as the central dualism through which the modern world is apprehended. Mitchell, following Heidegger, argues that once that distinction was in place, and reality standardly experienced as that which could be represented, as an exhibition open to the gaze of the (detached) observer, then we had moved from the 'exhibition of the world ... to the world conceived as though it were an exhibition' (Mitchell 1988: 13). This world is, according to Mitchell, distinguished by three key features:

First, its remarkable claim to certainty or truth: the apparent certainty with which everything seems ordered and organized, calculated and rendered unambiguous – ultimately, what seems its political decidedness. Second, the paradoxical nature of this decidedness: its certainty exists as the seemingly determined relation between representations and 'reality'; yet the real world, like the world outside the exhibition, despite everything the exhibition promises, turns out to consist only of further representations of this reality. Third, what I will refer to as its colonial nature: the age of the exhibition was necessarily the colonial age, the age of world economy and global power in

Figure 1 The island of La Cartuja
Source: Penelope Harvey

which we live, since what was to be rendered as exhibit was
reality, the world itself.

(Mitchell 1988: 13)

The nation state lies at the heart of this model of the world
and has been a primary agent in its production and perpetuation.
For, as Friedman has noted:

> The formation of the nation state in Europe was a systemic
> regional phenomenon and the nation state has been able to set
> the bounds for a certain kind of thinking about social process.
> Concepts such as society, national economy and people are all
> modeled on the existence of a homogenizing national entity.
> Ricardo's world was no less globalized than that of the six-
> teenth century or the twentieth, but he could represent it in
> terms of autonomous social units because of the local identity
> units into which it was constituted.

(Friedman 1994: 3)

One of the aims of this book is to consider the effects of
changing conceptualizations of the social and the cultural in a
world that has, according to many social theorists, moved from
the modern to the postmodern, from certainty to ambiguity, to the
self-conscious play with receding horizons and with paradox, to
a post-colonial world in which multiculturalism refigures (and
reconfirms) racial hierarchies and in which sociobiology is joined
by biosociality:

> If sociobiology is culture constructed on the basis of a metaphor
> of nature, then in biosociality, nature will be modeled on cul-
> ture understood as practice. Nature will be known and remade
> through technique and will finally become artificial, just as
> culture becomes natural. Were such a project to be brought to
> fruition, it would stand as the basis for overcoming the nature/
> culture split.

(Rabinow 1992: 241–2)

What is the world as exhibition in the late twentieth century?
And how is such a world presented? What are the relationships
between representation and reality in our contemporary world
where communications technologies have complicated the distinctions that we habitually made between representations and realities, where this relationship is itself the subject of observation,

where the dualities of the world have been challenged as much by our technological capacities as by our theoretical advances? What difference does it make that we live in a world where hybrid forms can appear to offer connections, where previously natural distinctions are no longer held to be absolute? How are the new hybrids doing the work that was previously done by the practices of categorical distinction? How is cultural (contingent) difference operating through the relations once defined by racial (absolute) differences?

THE GLOBAL AND THE LOCAL

The global economy of the late twentieth century produces paradoxes of scale. Massive integrated systems operate through the participation of ever less integrated components. Images of coherence that characterized previous global systems no longer predominate. The impressive architectural monuments that characterized the working of nineteenth century industrialism are no longer necessary for companies whose material presence might be no more than a box of contracts, the enumeration of those people who belong, temporarily and for the duration of a particular service, to the network which generates wealth and power for another equally disparate and dispersed group of investors.[3]

Within the nation state, devolution and a concern to develop local community exists alongside federalization and a desire to create economies of scale, and both operate simultaneously against what are seen by people of all political persuasions as the cumbersome bureaucracies of medium-scale units. In national museums there has been a move away from a concern with universalism, to a search for more localized knowledges. The general topic of humanity is not seen as one to attract the museum visiting public, who in turn are no longer addressed even as citizens of particular nations, but are increasingly catered for as individual consumers (Macdonald 1992b, 1993a). The move from citizen to consumer is also a visible outcome of the current ways in which nation states are objectified as institutions.

Contemporary cultural theory now necessarily involves some consideration of the relationship between the global and the local. This relationship has come to encompass the social realities of the late twentieth century, at least for those involved in reflecting on and writing about such things.[4] In anthropological circles it is increasingly accepted that 'all anthropology should be of the global' (Friedman 1994: 3), however localized the focus through which the ethnographer approaches the problem.[5] Contemporary modernities are presented as the effects of various globalizing processes, generally deemed to hold common origins in the imperial drives of powerful western institutions. Thus the processes of globalization are those manifested in, for example, flows of capital and credit, the interconnections afforded by new communications technologies, the speed of travel and increased mobility of populations, the immediacy of image and the consumerist promotion of mass-produced cultural forms. However, it is also acknowledged that once we start to look at embodied subjectivity, the effects of globalization are extremely diverse. The particularity of such outcomes thus provokes questions about the interdependence of continuity and change, homogenization and fragmentation.

However, the effects of these general social processes are not only 'out there', they are also implicit in the intellectual practices of the theorists themselves. For example we find this contrast of scale, the global and the local, as a particular division of labour both between and within academic disciplines, between those who pay attention to the universal (the global process) and those who look at the particular (the local effect).

The theorists are concerned to discuss the effects of contemporary capitalism (particularly what is viewed as its current crisis) and the changes in subjective awareness caused by the advent of mass media and information technologies. Thus Lyotard (1984) discusses the destabilization of reality, and the subsequent changes in the nature of human experience. Baudrillard argues for the increasing importance of consumption over production and the ways in which self-referential media images cause the proliferation of the banal.[6] Jameson (1984) discusses the joint demise of the modernist aesthetic and the bourgeois individual subject and shares with Harvey (1989) an interest in new experiences of space and time. Guattari urges us to look seriously into questions of subjectivity production in our present environment of 'deathlike entropy' (Guattari 1992: 36).

The ethnographers do not tend to work with these kinds of generalizations but are more concerned to discuss the complexities of specific contemporary subjectivities. Thus while some of the trends identified by the social and cultural theorists might inform their observations and even resonate with some of their findings, the pictures which they seek to produce are more textured and less categorical.[7]

The division between these two kinds of work points to a problem about the complementarity of ethnography and theory. It is a division of labour in which neither side is particularly convinced about the validity of what the other is engaged in. The theorists, presumably with greater cultural capital and less concern with their own status, tend to ignore rather than criticize ethnographic study. The distinction between the global and the local is treated as a difference in scale. The global is privileged as the more embracing, wider ranging perspective, the more complete approach which while it may be enriched with reference to the small-scale specificity of the ethnographic study, nevertheless works towards revealing the wider picture. In this view ethnography is the study of the particular (hence the terminology of the case study) while the theorists are those who produce more generalized abstractions, the context for local interactions. The ethnographers however have a different view of scale, and might in fact be more interested in how it is that parts and wholes are made to cohere, either in practice or in descriptions.[8] They are keen to show how shifts in scale do not involve a move between levels of complexity. In this sense there can be no such thing as a small-scale society or a complex society (common terms even among anthropologists). If 'society' is a way of designating processes, then forms of sociality cannot be reduced to metaphors of size or density (Strathern 1991a: xix).

There are thus complex issues at stake in the relationship between theory and ethnography. It is not simply a matter of the relationship between universals and particulars, or a debate over whether there is any chance of a dialogue between the general theorizers and those who look at specifics.[9] Anthropology is a discipline which has built itself around this issue after all, empirical ethnographic study constituting the comparative basis for theoretical models (western representations) of human social and cultural practice. The problem, from the anthropological side, seems to be a concern that the abstract theorizers actually produce false or meaningless generalizations because they do not ground their work in the specificity of actual lived practice but depend instead on introspection or text-based (secondary) accounts of practice. In this regard the ethnographic approach so central to anthropological practice, is not primarily about the specificity of the small-scale, but about the accuracy of that observed and experienced at first hand, what people actually say and do, as opposed to what certain cultural critics suppose 'people' (whoever they may be) to say and do. The contrast has been described as the distinction between the phenomenological and the textual approach to cultural practice, and is sometimes evoked as the fundamental distinction between an anthropological and a cultural studies approach.[10] The distinction is interesting to me given the circumstances of the Expo study which in many ways situated this work between anthropology and cultural studies in the terms discussed above.

In the first place the period of fieldwork on which this study was based was very short. Funding circumstances made prolonged participant observation impossible. In fact the project was funded so late in the day that there was no possibility of witnessing the whole event, yet alone being involved in the all-important prior stages of planning and organization. The Expo ran from April to October 1992 and we did not arrive there until late in August. In all I made three visits over the final three months of the fair and a further two trips in 1993. Obviously this was not a straightforward piece of participant observation. I found myself in a situation where the kind of research I was carrying out, while still ethnographic, was nevertheless of a kind that anthropologists tend to eschew. I was thus in a position to turn my attention, as an anthropologist, to the kind of knowledge that is generated by research methods which involve shorter term observation, less participation and more interviewing and textual analysis.

The second non-standard feature of my ethnographic practice was the research identity I adopted. Traditionally the ethnographer's research persona emerges in all its complexity, slowly, over time. The researcher expects to be taken as an outsider, as someone seeking some kind of local knowledge and marked out by their lack of understanding. Most researchers also gradually achieve relationships of inclusion as friends, family members, fellow workers, etc. Indeed many classic ethnographies begin with the tale of just how such incorporation was achieved, often by chance and without the explicit intention of the anthropologist.[11] Ethnographers' positioning involves the continual movement between the distance of the observer and the proximity of the participant. At the Expo these positions were confused in the sense that most visitors arrived from other places, and were at least initially unfamiliar with the practices of the Expo site. To stand outside and observe the world as exhibition was a crucial participatory activity. By the same token, given that the Expo site was designed for rapid consumption and many visitors spent only a few days there, the possibilities for increasing proximity through participation was complicated by the brevity of such visits. As it was I adopted the guise of a journalist.[12] The obvious and immediate advantages of this position were entirely practical and included the ease of access to informants from the production teams and the speed with which the exhibition could be visited. Journalists were quite central to the workings of the exhibition. They were encouraged to gather information about the event and disseminate it around the world. There were press officers in all the main pavilions to answer questions and provide background information, the press had free access to the fair and did not have to queue to visit the individual exhibits. The centrality of the press to this event was reflected in the architecture of the Press Centre, an imposing white marble building, one of the most impressive permanent structures of the Expo site.

As would any journalist, I also used sources other than those officially provided. My access to informants was better than it might have been thanks to those chance happenings which affect the ways in which most ethnographic work is carried out. On my very first day on the site I discovered, in the process of trying to secure a press pass, that two friends were working in relatively influential positions in the Expo management. One of these friends had been employed by the Expo to ensure the participation of many of the African and South American nation states and subsequently to direct one of the main exhibition spaces. The other was responsible for liaising between a particular group of national participants and the Expo management. Through him I learnt about details of personnel, VIP visits, the organization of taxes, concessions and diplomatic work. Between them my friends made it possible for me to meet people who were not explicitly briefed to talk to the press. I thus worked openly as a journalist, I had a somewhat indirect experience of certain of the management processes through watching and talking to these friends, I had interviews and casual conversations with many different kinds of people working at the Expo and finally there was always that informal off-the-record information gleaned by simply 'hanging out', watching and listening to what went on around me as I spent my days visiting the exhibits and sitting or walking around the exhibition site. I talked to people who had visited the exhibition and last but not least I read and watched much of the massive textual coverage of the event produced by the local, national and international media.

The status of the ethnographic observer is central to anthropological self-definitions and to adopt the role of journalist might well be seen by some as sufficient to jeopardize the production of an anthropological account. Bourdieu (1984a: 3) has identified the journalist as one who 'inhabits the borderland between scholarly and ordinary knowledge', and one who has a stake in 'blurring the frontier and denying or eliminating what separates scientific analysis from partial objectifications'. Ironically Bourdieu's formulation might well be taken as an incentive to adopt the journalistic stance by anyone worried about the unthinking imposition of the representational model with its associated detached observer. On the other hand an obvious problem with journalism is the association of the practice with a vision of the world as external reality, that which can be represented, that which presents itself as an exhibit before an observer (Mitchell 1988: 29). In such practice the observing subject stands apart from the world and observes and represents but in his or her own image. But as in anthropology the journalist wants to be there, to know through experience:

> While setting themselves apart . . . from the world as picture, Europeans also wanted to experience it as though it were the real thing. Like the visitor to an exhibition, travellers wanted to immerse themselves in the Orient and 'touch with their fingers a strange civilisation'. . . . There is a contradiction between the need to separate oneself from the world and render it up as an object of representation, and the desire to lose oneself within this object-world and experience it directly; a contradiction which world exhibitions were built to accommodate and overcome.
>
> (Mitchell 1988: 29)

Anthropological practice certainly inhabits this paradox, but can use it self-consciously to develop a critical method. For while anyone reading this book can recognize the world as exhibition, it can also be recognized that others do not necessarily see the world in this way and nor indeed do we. For the world is not simply picture, even at an exhibition. So, what difference did my status as a journalist make to my study? Did it render my work non-anthropological? Is the primary difference between anthropology and journalism one of method, of expertise, or of objective? The anthropology that emerged from the study of the Expo'92 could not reproduce the classic genre of an account of cultural 'others', but it did enable consideration of the relationship between this more standard kind of anthropological knowledge and that produced in the alternative ethnographic genres of anthropology at home, auto-anthropology and cultural studies.

ETHNOGRAPHY OF THE CULTURALLY FAMILIAR

Ethnography of the culturally familiar poses very interesting problems for anthropologists whose analytical tradition has predominantly favoured the task of describing and analysing cultural difference. To study what is already known creates problems of relative expertise. Who knows best, anthropologist, academic audience or the research subjects themselves? How are these various knowledges conflated or brought together in anthropological accounts? Anthropology at home has tended to confront this problem by stressing the cultural distance between researcher and researched. Thus urban intellectuals study rural communities, middle-class academics work with poor or immigrant communities. The tradition of separation is common in European anthropology. As Herzfeld writes: 'Mediterranean anthropology has created a need for exoticizing devices to justify research in what is otherwise a familiar cultural backyard' (Herzfeld 1987: 11).[13]

The production of the ethnographic monograph is another such device through which ethnographers of the familiar align themselves with more traditional ethnography to create otherness through the distancing mechanisms of representational practice (Boon 1982, Said 1978). Such practice is central to anthropology's own cultural background and once recognized, it increasingly became a focus for cultural analysis in its own right.[14] Herzfeld has made the point that this trend for reflexivity was welcomed by many as an antidote to the exoticism that had previously been a necessary feature of doing anthropology at home (Herzfeld 1987: 3).

Auto-anthropology was the term coined by Strathern to refer

to 'anthropology carried out in the context which produced it' (Strathern 1987a: 17), a mode of analysis that draws on concepts which belong to the society or culture under study and cannot depend on the more usual appeal to concepts of difference and incommensurability or the provocation of culture shock (Wagner 1975) which defines so much anthropological practice (Strathern 1987b). Strathern's own ethnographic work has stressed the importance of an anthropological recognition of the possibility of incommensurability between cultures, to the extent that culture itself as a knowable entity is depicted as an effect of western thought and knowledge practices (Strathern 1988). Indeed it is not coincidental, although I acknowledge that this is probably a particularly British perspective, that those working in areas such as Melanesia and more recently Amazonia, see themselves as the most radical contemporary theorizers of the discipline. The ability to use ethnographic study to throw western analytic concepts into relief does not require an absolute belief in cultural relativism, as some have tried to argue, but it does require an ethnographic focus on difference. This is more easily achieved in some parts of the world than others, and is most definitely not available at an event such as Expo'92, nor at many of the other events we describe as products of mass popular culture. What we learn as anthropologists, from participation in these events, must therefore be of a different order from what we might learn through participation in the daily practices of a place such as Mount Hagen. If ethnography is our best shot at breaking out of reiteration,[15] where does that leave the auto-anthropologist?

The Expo'92 was a prime candidate for 'auto-anthropology'. If culture and social organization are the main conceptual concerns of the discipline and provide the language through which anthropologists go about their business, then a cultural event concerned to display the existence and connection between nation states, the environment and the global economy, was treading very similar ground.

What is it though that distinguishes an anthropological approach to such matters from that espoused in the growing field of cultural studies? The institutional relationship between cultural studies and social anthropology in the UK is perhaps responsible for the negative feelings that cultural studies provoke in some anthropologists. Growing as it did from the concerns of English scholars engaged in the analysis of text and concentrating on the cultural effects of the politics of class, race and gender, cultural studies was adopted most avidly by those seeking to radicalize the methods and concerns of the humanities by applying the insights of social and cultural theory.[16] Anthropology's traditional commitment to the study of cultural difference is one reason for the reluctance that some have shown to embrace cultural studies. However, many of those who attack the cultural studies approach focus on the differences between studying texts and studying people, between representation and situated practice.

This characterization overlooks the fact that some of the greatest exponents of the textual approach have themselves been anthropologists, Clifford Geertz being perhaps the most well-known,[17] and the fact that the critique of a textualist approach is voiced by leading exponents of cultural studies:

> Identity could be seen as dragging cultural studies into the 1990s by acting as a kind of guide to how people see themselves, not as class subjects, not as psychoanalytic subjects, not as subjects of ideology, not as textual subjects, but as active agents whose sense of self is projected onto and expressed in an expansive range of cultural practices, including texts, images, and commodities . . . . The site of identity formation in cultural studies remains implicitly in and through cultural commodities and texts rather than in and through the cultural practices of everyday life . . . it is necessary that we somehow move away from the binary opposition which still haunts cultural studies, that is, the distinction between text and lived experience, between media and reality, between culture and society.
>
> (McRobbie 1992: 730)

As McRobbie's plea indicates, awareness of a tension between text and everyday practice is not exclusively anthropological. Cultural theorists of many kinds might want to address these issues. The critiques that anthropologists make of those who treat cultural practice as representational, or of those who reduce culture to text, harks back to the critique of linguistic models of signification. To make this critique is to invoke a particular understanding and trajectory of 'culture', as an objectified unit of analysis. Thus we find 'culture' as something separated from everyday life through a particular regime of representation (such as art), and following on this separation comes the rising importance of specialist knowledge (the official, legitimized interpreters), and then a subsequent fragmentation of knowledge as a result of challenges to claims to expertise, and finally the increasing interest in popular culture and more democratic regimes of representation where all can interpret. It is interesting that while many contemporary anthropologists attribute such a model to those working within the field of cultural studies, it could also be taken as a more general history of western notions of culture and one which has been traversed by anthropologists as well as other cultural theorists. The twist is that anthropological interest in everyday practice, while long-standing, was also the hallmark of anthropological expertise. The tenuous nature of such expertise has become unavoidably visible now that other cultural theorists are working the same territory.

ANTHROPOLOGY AND CULTURAL STUDIES

I am intrigued by the problematic relationship between social anthropology and cultural studies. While it is most definitely the case that many have embraced this possibility for interdisciplinary work, others are busy putting up the barricades. Few anthropologists in favour of using cultural studies as a source of cultural theory have explicitly addressed the issue of the compatibility of theoretical approach. In a more personal way I have seen how the 'problem' with cultural studies lies behind local intellectual skirmishes, at conferences and occasionally in journals, even determining whether the work of certain trained anthropologists is considered sufficiently anthropological for them to take up lectureships in the discipline. I have felt genuinely bewildered by the strength of feeling that these largely unacknowledged confrontations have evoked. These circumstances are among my motivations for writing this book. I feel very strongly that the discipline of anthropology cannot ignore the contributions from cultural studies.

Furthermore the hostility which the cultural studies style of interdisciplinarity evokes is itself revealing. The aversion shown to cultural studies is not extended to other disciplines, such as history for example, despite the fact that many contemporary historians quite self-consciously write in conversation with some of the major cultural theorists espoused by cultural studies.[18] Those French cultural theorists who Bourdieu refers to as the heresiarchs (Barthes, Deleuze, Derrida, Foucault, and the minor heresiarchs Baudrillard and Lyotard) (Bourdieu 1984a: xxv), are all characterized by their dual relationship with philosophy and social science, and are in some ways problematic for anthropology because of a tendency (apparently)[19] to produce philosophical generalization from culturally specific foundations. But the ethnocentrism of social theory is not new, so why this particular concern with alternative forms of theorizing from within a discipline which has always drawn its social theory from beyond its own empirical fields of expertise? And why now?

Cultural theory is a growth industry in academic circles, as are the related more empirical concerns of cultural studies. If cultural studies is problematic because of its ubiquity, its popularity, what exactly is under threat? What is anthropology aiming to preserve or protect and how might we seek to value what the cultural studies approach is obviously offering to so many scholars without sacrificing the specificity of the anthropological approach? Is such a marriage possible? Is it desirable?

One obvious problem lies with the concept of 'culture' itself. Its use as a specialized concept for the generation of anthropological theory or the focus of ethnographic enquiry has been undermined by ethnographic studies that are not concerned with what anthropologists understand as cultural matters.[20] The more serious problem, which accounts for the possibility of the first, is the ubiquity of the term itself, its simultaneous visibility and taken-for-granted status in particular western discourses, such that empirical studies of whatever kind by definition attend to cultural practice. The rub lies in the fact that this visibility seems to mimic the specialized domain that anthropology has elaborated over the past century.

These concerns are not trivial. There is quite legitimate worry about the ways in which concepts such as 'cultural difference' are used in political conflicts to justify practices such as 'ethnic cleansing' in the Balkan conflict, or the ways in which the British Government has invoked an equivalence between 'individual' and 'society' in order to abdicate social responsibility and deny the prior existence of relationships (Ingold 1990). As cultural theorists, anthropologists are concerned about their complicity in, if not responsibility for, such effects, mindful of the ways in which this has occurred in the past.[21]

Another problem lies with the study of particular western practices, which tend to get bracketed together as mass popular culture. Empirical cultural studies are interested in football, in department stores, theme parks, tourism and particularly with the media, television, magazines and advertising.[22] As mass cultural forms, these are the products of the consumer industries which are themselves largely responsible for the appropriation, 'globalization' and naturalization of 'culture'. As obvious constructs, outcomes of particular commercial interests, these cultural forms seem less authentic, less embodied than those with which anthropologists have traditionally been concerned. Yet these practices involve millions of people? What might anthropology have to say about these people. If anthropology is philosophy with the people in (Ingold 1992), does it matter which people? If anthropologists study mass popular culture, do their analyses look different from those grounded in, say, sociology or cultural studies?

These theoretical and empirical concerns are very closely linked in the four central chapters of this book. Our theoretical tools, of whichever discipline or interdisciplinary combination, emerge from the particular circumstances of western academic production and are thus inextricable from the conceptual processes which produce and support parallel western institutions. As Bourdieu (1984a) has suggested, western academic practice itself necessarily brings together embodied everyday experience and abstracted representational forms, even if only by virtue of the fact that academic production requires readers, whose acts of interpretation consistently undermine academic claims to expertise. Anthropology, as the discipline which has long argued for the embeddedness of cultural forms, is thus inevitably implicated in mass popular culture in ways that merit investigation. The anthropology of 'other cultures' has always attempted to integrate the theorizations of local 'intellectuals' (often identified as key informants) with observation of daily practice and particular public ceremonial or festivity. The link is fundamental to anthropological practice, the tracing of analogies between domains a distinguishing feature.

It is with the above concerns in mind, that I embark on a discussion of three modernist western institutions: the discipline of social anthropology, the nation state, and the universal exhibition. The histories of these institutions are well documented and their comparison, over time, thus enables a substantive discussion of some of the claims that cultural theorists are making concerning the degree and the speed of change in our contemporary social world. Furthermore, these institutions are linked by their concern with the relationship between the universal and the particular, and by their quite explicit engagement in the uniquely modernist practice of the objectification of culture.

As discussed above, I was unable to observe or participate in the practice of setting up the Expo'92. What was available for observation was the relationship between the representational practices employed by the nation states and the multinationals, and those used by myself as anthropologist, as we all, in related but different ways, worked to reveal the cultural. Traditionally an ethnographic study of participation in a mass event would lead the anthropologist to identify with particular people and their immediate communities. Through participant observation the anthropologist would seek to contextualize the lived experience of participation in the event in terms of other aspects of people's lives. The interviews would not generally be taken as a suitable method to generate contextual knowledge precisely because of the assumption of a crucial gap between representation and everyday practice. This method has been used to great effect in the recent work of Macdonald and Bouquet. Macdonald worked with the planners of an exhibit on food at London's Science Museum (Macdonald 1992a) while Bouquet has written a reflexive account of her own role in setting up an exhibit on the representation of kinship (Bouquet 1995b). Both these writers give fascinating accounts of the complex intentions that precede the staging of major exhibits, the processes through which these are negotiated, the ambiguities and compromises entailed in the final forms and the ways in which visitors interpret what is presented to them. In both cases the focus of the ethnography is on the planners and the processes through which particular exhibits emerge.

Alternatively I could have focused on the Expo visitor. My anthropological training did provoke moments of guilt about not queuing, often for up to eight hours at a time, to enter a single pavilion, and *experiencing* the exhibition as any other visitor might. However, I soon realized that to have focused on the experience of such consumers would simply have led me to learn something 'else' about the event, not something more valid, more definitive of its nature, let alone something more anthropological. In any event of this size (there were 45 million visits made over the six-month period), there is a tension for the ethnographer who has to decide what exactly to participate in, but this was not the problem. Anthropologists have studied participation in mass cultural events for many decades. The anthropology of pilgrimage provides an apt model for the study of a world fair, as pilgrimage centres have frequently been described as market places for more than spiritual exchange. I did not take this perspective but chose to focus on the parallel discourses of the Expo visitors, cultural theory and an ethnographically motivated anthropology. I thus decided to incorporate anthropology as part of the ethnographic object that was to become the focus of my research. As Herzfeld has noted, studies of Euro-American society rarely contemplate anthropological epistemology as an ethnographic object. To do so is to muddy the categorical distinction that privileges academic discourse over its object (Herzfeld 1987: 15). It is my contention that one of the difficulties the discipline has with auto-anthropology, as a distinctive ethnographic genre, arises from the blurring of distinctions between representation and practice which occur once we begin to look at the self-conscious production of culture.

A consideration of the distinctions drawn between the representational and the embodied, or what Bourdieu has termed the scientific and the everyday, is itself a consideration of social relations and the workings of creative and/or coercive power. What we often present as abstract theoretical concerns are simultaneously embedded in very concrete social practices. This division between a representational and a practice approach is thus a problematic dichotomy and one which sustains what I see as an unnecessary breach between anthropology and cultural studies. In general terms my study thus became defined as one which looks at the generation and representation of knowledge in the universal exhibition and in the discipline of anthropology around the concepts of the nation and national culture.

THE EXPO'92

The concrete focal point for these discussions is the Expo'92, the last universal exhibition of the twentieth century, which was held in Seville from 20 April until 12 October 1992. One hundred and twelve nation states accepted the Spanish monarch's invitation to participate, and each was encouraged to produce displays of artistic, cultural and scientific achievement which referred to both the

Figure 2 The bridges across the Guadalquivir
Source: Expo'92 Official Guide

developments of the previous 500 years and the projected hopes
and expectations for the twenty-first century. In addition to the

national participants there were displays by international organizations and corporate participants, as well as theme pavilions and
entertainment venues and attractions.[23] The holding of universal
exhibitions is a competitive affair in which nations bid to host
the event in much the same way as they do to hold the Olympic
Games. Hosting nations have to show themselves capable of providing the necessary infrastructure to enable the event to run
smoothly.[24] Host nations are also expected to produce extravagant
architectural statements, monuments to the event which will thus
continue in public awareness far beyond the short exhibition
period. The six bridges across the Guadalquivir River were
Spain's central contribution in this respect (Figure 2). The exhibition was held on the island of La Cartuja, an arid site which
the organizers reclaimed for the city with an appropriate symbolic
narrative:

> The reclamation of La Cartuja and its integration into the city
> could be seen as effecting on a small, symbolic scale what
> Expo'92 is proposing to the rest of the world. Here, against
> the backdrop of a city redolent of mixed cultures, on this
> once arid area, now landscaped and fully equipped with ultra-
> modern infrastructures, stands Expo'92.
>
> (Expo'92 Official Guide: 22)

Just as the bridges were the visible links to the city of Seville,
highly contemporary in form, symbolic of the hopes for future
connections, so too at the heart of the island was a building
designated as the symbolic focus for the reclamation of a glorious
past and even, coincidentally, for a passing allusion to the industrial revolution of the nineteenth century (Figure 3):

> The nerve centre of the Universal Exposition is La Cartuja, the
> fifteenth century Carthusian monastery which gives its name to
> the island formed between two branches of the River Guad-
> alquivir. Columbus is known to have stayed in the monastery
> and later, in the nineteenth century, a china factory was built
> here: its slender chimneys still stand. The complex is now the
> home of the Royal Pavilion for Expo'92, now the focal point of
> Expo'92, this complex of history-steeped buildings encapsulates
> both innovation and tradition.
>
> (Expo'92 Official Guide: 44)

Expo'92 was granted universal status by the International Bureau of Expositions.[25] Universal and international expositions are differentiated on the basis of the scope of the organizing theme, the catchment of participants and the autonomy of their displays. The highest status is reserved for those fairs with the greatest ambition for totalization. The Expo'92 in Seville certainly earned its universal status in this respect. Its general thematic focus was 'The Age of Discoveries' and the organizers produced the rhetoric for a massive stock-taking of the modern age. King Juan Carlos of Spain welcomed visitors with these words:

> The turn of the century is a time for assessing the past and tackling the future. And this is exactly what the Seville 1992 Universal Exposition does: it is at once a digest and a preview. In celebrating the achievements of the human race, it also celebrates our hitherto untapped potential. Seville provides a link between the past and the future, considers each in the light of the other, and intertwines the two in a way that illuminates the issues of our time.
>
> (Expo'92 Official Guide: 13)

The exhibition thus positioned itself quite self-consciously between a future marked by the approaching millennium and the quincentennial anniversary of Columbus' voyage to the New World in 1492.

Expo'92 thus had its own particular agenda, and its form was in many ways influenced by the concerns of Spain, the host nation. However it also stands as an excessive example of otherwise ubiquitous institutions and practices. As Ames remarked concerning Montreal's Expo'86: 'Expo reproduced at the concrete level of common sense the essential features of a modern capitalist society' (Ames 1992: 130). Hyper-modernism, enterprise culture, heritage and tourist industries, the architecture and relationships of movement were all encapsulated in its forms. It produced an exaggerated version of what we have become accustomed to in such cultural stopping points as airports and motorway service stations in which high-tech capitalism harnesses the potentials and images of space travel while a cynical rationalization of modernism simultaneously sells people heritage 'authenticity'.[26] It was notable that among the numerous 'producers' of Expo'92 were many who were quite conscious of this fact and enjoyed the games and jokes which this awareness afforded.

Figure 3 The Carthusian monastery of La Cartuja
Source: Penelope Harvey

Expo'92 was a highly reflexive, self-conscious event and worked with the paradoxes and problems which its modernist foundations have produced.

As with previous exhibitions, the producers of Expo'92 explicitly set out to demonstrate and display the radical effects of human progress and innovation. Yet to do so, of course, they needed simultaneously to sustain a sense of continuity, perhaps most importantly a continuity of the very modernist premises through which a cultural form such as the universal exhibition is sustained. These comparative possibilities are implicit in the ways in which the Expo presented itself and existed as an entity which we might compare with earlier similar events. Such continuities were also quite explicit, visible components of the Expo display. Particular national and corporate exhibits made reference to earlier world fairs as did the massive textual and audio-visual commentary.

While Expo as an institution can be described and analyzed in terms of its particular historical trajectory and contemporary form, it is also an event which challenges the theories and methods of anthropology by working with the same conceptual tools as those with which we as anthropologists seek to comprehend. Chapter 2 uses the notion of auto-anthropology (Strathern 1987b) to raise questions about what happens when culture and context become explicit, and to focus explicitly on institutions (the exhibition, the nation state, cultural theory) that have embraced the possibility of treating culture as representation, of acknowledging the world as exhibition.

To look at these relationships as an anthropologist, is, of course, to jump through the looking glass, and eschew certainties, closures, even clarifications. The Expo'92 is an institution close to home, analyzed in order to explore 'the complicity of being involved in its social game', what Bourdieu has termed the *illusio* – that which creates both 'the value of the objectives of the game, as it does the value of the game itself' (Bourdieu 1984a: xii). In taking this approach I also consider the extent to which anthropology, as a 'technology of knowledge', merely mimics the effects of other more powerful contemporary institutions. The Expo'92 offered two intriguing possibilities in this respect. First it offered an example of explicit, self-conscious cultural practice. To do anthropology at the Expo not only involved recovering the implicit from observed practice but also entailed the observation of people self-consciously engaged in producing and representing culture. Second, when taken in historical perspective, the Expo material engaged in a concrete way with many of the abstract discussions and debates about the relationship between modernity and postmodernity and the effects that this relationship might have on the generation of cultural practice.

The relationship between culture and the nation state is discussed in Chapter 3. The display of national cultures has since the turn of the century been the most general organizing principle of world fairs, although the understanding of cultural difference that such displays entail has changed during the course of this century. The great exhibitions of the late nineteenth and early twentieth centuries specifically aimed to promote the need for the domination of foreign markets, to make modernity unthinkable without colonialism. The lavish display of both exotic goods and the products of a burgeoning manufacturing industry were designed to provoke interest and admiration and enlist public support for the political economy of colonialism. Colonized nations were to provide both raw materials and markets for manufactured goods in an exchange that was presented as to the benefit of all. The exploration of cultural difference in national institutions such as museums, exhibitions and indeed academic disciplines such as anthropology, would provide choice, possibilities for progress and regeneration.[27]

In the early twentieth century colonized peoples were displayed at world fairs to provide, through contrastive effect, visual evidence of the evolution of civilized nations (Rydell 1984). Culture was thus the visible effect of racial difference. In the exhibitions of the 1990s culture, tradition and identity continue to differentiate nation states, but these differences are no longer grounded in biological idioms of race. Chapter 3 traces a move from biological to cultural essentialism and discusses the ways in which this change can be identified in many domains of contemporary cultural practice and is also a feature of changing notions of culture within social anthropology.[28] One of the arguments put forward is that while national participants in world fairs at the turn of the century were, it appears, seeking to promote a coherent ideology that might 'confirm, extend and reconstitute the authority and values of the centre of society' (Rydell 1984: 2),[29] it is now choice rather than coherence that participants seek to display. Nation states may still need to show themselves as 'socially progressive, morally virtuous, and technologically sophisticated' (Ames 1992: 113), but to do so no longer requires either the coherence or consistency of previous modernist paradigms.

Chapter 4 looks at the relationship between corporate and national participants at the Expo'92, as expressed through the use and presentation of 'technology' and 'culture'. As temporary yet monumental exhibits, world fairs are extremely flexible institutions of display. Unlike museums they can operate as sites of innovation and provide opportunities for the demonstration of new technologies and their effects.[30] Change and progress however are only visible in a context which also marks continuities and traditions. Thus although the idioms of power in Expo'92 were quite openly directed to a corporate model of the nation state, to the global competition for markets and control of the most advanced information technologies, the values of culture, tradition and identity were also emphasized. Nation states were produced as cultural entities in Expo'92 through the juxtaposition of innovation and tradition. Technology played a crucial role in this process and influenced the terms on which participants competed in this theatre of global display. The use of film technologies by the national and transnational participants was particularly important. Deleuze has argued that '[i]n the final analysis, the screen, as the frame of frames, gives a common standard of measurement to things which do not have one ... the frame ensures a deterritorialisation of the image' (Deleuze 1983/1986: 14–15). The ways in which film technologies operated to render nations equivalent and to reproduce hierarchies of difference in cultural rather than racial idioms are also discussed.

Consumers and citizens are the focus of Chapter 5 as I consider the effects of the exhibits on those for whom they were produced. In this discussion abstract theories of consumption, produced by writers such as Baudrillard and de Certeau are analyzed in the light of the practices of consumption observed at the Expo'92. Particular attention is paid to the role of the realist aesthetic, whose demise is not only much heralded by these theorists but is thought to have a radical effect on the subjectivities of consumers, and on understandings of knowledge. The other central argument of this chapter concerns the concept of experience. It is argued that at the Expo'92 'experience' itself was both simulated and commodified with the effect that representational practice can no longer simply be contrasted to embodied practice.

However it is also clear that visitors to the Expo were more than consumers, and in this respect the ethnographic material does modify the vision of cultural change suggested by, for example, Baudrillard.

By Chapter 6 I hope to have established that anthropology does have something particular to offer to the study of mass popular culture as the social science most fascinated by the cultural specificity of its own conceptual apparatus. For now it is important merely to note that this claim to particularity is based neither in method nor scale, but on conceptual approach, and it is the processes of conceptualization which I hope to reveal or make explicit through the various chapters.

HYBRIDS OF MODERNITY

For those who contend that postmodernism is an excess of modernism, hybrids are useful figures, the product of a modernity that has become self-conscious. No longer ensnared by their own fictions, hybrids can recognize their own multiplicity. In some scenarios they are used as figures of contestation, revealing the fact that modernist strategies for purification and rational classification generate their own excess, creating the conditions of self-awareness for those who do not fit. Colonized subjects answer back, feminist scholarship challenges from the margins, gay and lesbian subjects undermine accepted gender dichotomies. The power of the hybrid metaphor comes from its flouting of 'a static notion of identity that has been the core of cultural thought during the era of imperialism' (Said 1993: xxviii). However the hybrid, like the cyborg, metaphorically evokes both hope and menace. Its beginnings are neither innocent nor disinterested, let alone authentic or pure (Haraway 1991). The hybrid can only emerge from particular and political circumstances in which discontinuities have been deliberately staged and policies of categorical purification enacted, it is itself an effect of colonial power (Bhabha 1985). The problem is how to remain aware of the kinds of difference that particular hybrids connect and the effects of such connections.[31] These differences, which the concept of the hybrid both contains and obscures, are the subject of Young's careful discussion of the history of this term (Young 1995). Young points out, for example, that 'the hybrid' was the term used by the Victorian extreme right to put forward their ideas of species distinctions among humans (Young 1995: 10). He shows how the physiological hybrids of the nineteenth century are, in the twentieth century, characterized as cultural entities.

Young's examination of the historical genealogy of the hybrid has important implications for the move from nineteenth century models of racial difference to the cultural differences of the twentieth century:

> Hybridity . . . shows the connections between the racial categories of the past and contemporary cultural discourse: it may be used in different ways, given different inflections and apparently discrete references, but it always reiterates and reinforces the dynamics of the same conflictual economy whose tensions and divisions it re-enacts in its own antithetical structure . . . . Racial theory was never simply scientific or biologistic, just as its categories were never wholly essentializing. Today it is common to claim that in such matters we have moved from biologism and scientism to the safety of culturalism, that we have created distance and surety by the very act of the critique of essentialism and the demonstration of its impossibility: but that shift has not been so absolute, for the racial was always cultural, the essential never unequivocal.
>
> (Young 1995: 27–8)

My invocation of the hybrid is thus not to the figures on the margins but to the effects of the politics of exclusion within key modernist institutions. As hybrids, the nation state, the universal exhibition and the discipline of social anthropology are related, as it is through them that the racial differences which operate through discourses of multiculturalism and which emerge in the processes of unification and difference reproduce the possibilities for hybrid forms. As with all hybrid forms, however, these institutions do also contain the possibilities for effects not contained by original expectations. This book seeks to plot some of these effects in contemporary cultural theory.

Chapter 2

Anthropology: can we do anthropology when culture and context become self-evident?

CONTEXT AND THE CULTURAL CONSTRUCT[1]

Context and interpretation have a problematic status in contemporary cultural analysis. Theories of knowledge, concepts of truth and authenticity, modes of description and interpretation have been shaken by the critiques of certain forms of modernist scholarship, particularly those that advocate the general application of abstracted theoretical entities. In some disciplines such as history and sociology this challenge to the flattening effect of generalized theoretical context has been met by the (re)introduction of the concept of culture, above all to explain the differing outcomes of modernization and to account for its subjective, interpretive aspects.[2] This 'cultural turn' introduced a consideration of the dynamics of everyday life and operated as a force to reformulate traditional disciplinary concerns (Robertson 1992).

With regard to culture, anthropologists have a somewhat different trajectory behind them. In this discipline there is a concern that the concept of culture has become a liability, over-homogenizing, too static, an effect of description rather than its precondition. Nevertheless it is a concept which seems hard to dispose of, lying as it does at the heart of the anthropological endeavour:

> Culture is construed as a repository of information, explicit in the techniques of ethnomethodologists whose entry into another culture is through acquiring the tools of 'knowing how' to operate within its categories. The goal is to uncover ground rules, templates, codes, structures as information-bearing devices. The concept of culture thus demarcates the distinctiveness of the kind of information needed to be a member of a particular group, enclave, institution.... All societies thus

'have' culture, and the 'how to' rules and practices by which people conduct their lives afford an unwitting reservoir of information for the outsider. It is because we think that all societies have cultures, that we can play one off against another, engage in comparison, and ultimately use one's own culture as a foil for understanding others.

(Strathern 1987b: 30)

It is a commonplace of anthropological discourse to understand the objectification of social knowledge in rules and norms, as cultural constructs. Constructs are by their very nature partial, and the knowledge required to make sense of them is contextual. There is always something else that can be revealed from another perspective. In this sense forms are never complete but can always be added to through thicker and thicker description, increasing the layers of contextualization.

The awareness of culture as construct in turn provoked reflection on the constructed nature of anthropologists' own cultural products. People began to study the processes through which ethnographic knowledge emerges as such[3] and the ways in which contextual knowledge entails its own power, a power which can imply a degree of control by the knower over the known.[4] Anthropologists now have to deal with the awareness that the objectifications of ethnographic monographs are at best partial, at worst erroneous and misleading representations. Indeed, those who criticize the interventionist nature of anthropological practice, seek merely to move the site of its critical effect from the researched to the researching community. The consistent feature, integral to all academic practice, is that new knowledge is established in relation to, and often in refutation of, previous expertise (Bourdieu 1984a). Thus radicals and reactionaries fight in similar ways as they seem to establish particular foundational assumptions, interpretative possibilities and issues of adequate contextualization. Nor are these processes particular to the production and exchange of academic knowledge. Processes of contextualization and recontextualization are themselves aspects of communicative activity more generally, and such interactions are always imbued with the effects of power. Thus, for the partial construct to operate as knowledge, authorization and the establishment of expertise is required.

The construct has another implication. People study the cultural construction of sexuality, childhood, death, economy, kinship, etc. Such formulations assume an inherent point of comparison as the analyst examines how stable entities take particular forms. Thus, cultural constructionism posits cultural difference but not incommensurability. I will argue that this aspect of the concept of culture as construct is analagous to the outcomes of commodification processes in the worlds of advertising and entertainment, where difference proliferates but where there is no hint of incommensurability.[5] As culture becomes ubiquitous so too does context, and as culture becomes increasingly reflexive, so too the context implodes.

Third, the notion of culture as construct carries a connotation of intentionality and has often been linked to the assumption that cultural practices, and particularly cultural artefacts, are intrinsically communicative and that the task of the cultural analyst is to recover these meanings through interpretation.[6] This is the world as exhibition in which semiosis is taken as a universal condition (Mitchell 1988: 14). An alternative approach is to look at what cultural practice does, to study situated effects rather than attempting to recover cognitive schema.[7] These positions emerge from decades of debate on the relationship between system and practice, representation and experience, but the issue is not trivial and returns us to the necessity of some kind of appeal to context. For as soon as we engage in the *description* of cultural effects, inevitably interpretative, provisional and partial, we call forth the necessity of contextualization, the need to explain the cultural and social preconditions for such effects. Anthropological practice thus requires contextualization. However, the practices which anthropologists describe are not necessarily adequately represented in these terms. Thus we find a further effect of descriptive partiality, a concern with the nature of the gaps and spaces that descriptions produce.

One such gap, which is the subject of recent writings by Strathern, is that which emerges from the comparison between different ways of knowing. Strathern's work suggests that for Melanesians, culture emerges from deconstruction or decomposition rather than construction. Collective activities, clan engagements, initiation rituals are effective to the extent that they take pre-existing social relations apart (Strathern 1992a). Cultural practice is directed to eliciting particular partial forms. Cultural entities are ontologically whole, they contain other versions of themselves and the cultural process involves effectively producing particular versions of that whole in social interactions. Thus fragmentation of the body/person/clan is an explicit aim of particular kinds of exchange. For these (remarkably Lacanian) subjects, cultural work is about deconstructing merged/total unreproductive entities, about creating difference rather than achieving social unity.[8] Euro-Americans place the emphasis elsewhere. In this understanding of cultural practice, it is the connections, not the separations, which are achieved. Separation is deemed problematic.

My argument has come full circle in an attempt to show that contemporary problems with context and interpretation are intimately related to the notion of culture as construct. It is modernist notions of the construct, of knowledge through progressive accumulation, of a particular relationship between representation and truth, which have created the conditions for its own collapse. Strathern's distinction between Melanesian and western forms of sociality can thus be taken as a heuristic device to indicate an important contrast between approaches which posit ontological wholeness and see cultural practice as directed to fragmentation ('Melanesian'), and those which posit ontological fragmentation and see cultural practice as directed to building, construction and accumulation ('Western'). The distinction is itself a partial construct, and as a heuristic device can be made to operate within as well as between social entities. In recent discussions of the ways in which distinctions are drawn in practice, Strathern (1991b) and Wagner (1991) have stressed that the contrast also operates within what have been bounded as Melanesian or western domains. Similar arguments on the effects of scale in relation to the kinds of knowledge we produce have also been made by Latour, who claims that the West has never been *modern* (Latour 1993). He argues that it is the ability to invoke situationally a temporal and transformational dimension to the nature/culture, science/politics and truth/value dichotomies that has sustained western political and scientific dominance. It is in the spirit of revealing the interdependence of the terms of such oppositions that I have invoked the distinctions between 'Western' and 'Melanesian' understandings of culture and context. The exercise also serves to reveal the centrality of the construct for anthropological practice, and opens up the possibility of discussing the implicit dimensions of power in the relationship between interpretation and knowledge.

My attempt to study Expo'92 raised interesting questions about how to locate/limit 'context' and about the kind of knowledge interpretation affords. In many ways the Expo'92 research exemplified why it is that 'context' constitutes a problem for contemporary social theory, and perhaps particularly for social anthropology. In the next section of this chapter the heuristic role of both context and interpretation for the generation of anthropological knowledge will be considered. A guiding concern is to illustrate the difference between (i) the idea that knowledge/ understanding is achieved via contextualization, a process in which additional information is brought to bear from outside and beyond the interaction itself, and (ii) the idea that knowledge/ understanding is achieved via interaction and concrete situated practice, that things are known in terms of their consequences and that cultural entities are always in process. The distinction is analogous to that drawn by Mitchell who contrasts the western representational model used by French engineers with Bourdieu's description of the Kabyle understanding of their dwellings. For the former things are known by virtue of detached, outside observations and the fixing or ordering of practice in rules, structures and meanings, while for the latter knowledge of the world emerges in their daily lives:

> The order of the Kabyle house, or what we would call the organisation of its space (none of these terms is sufficient or appropriate) can better be thought of as this kind of attentiveness to the world's fertility or potential fullness. Such potential or force plays as the rhythm of life, a life made up not of inert objects to be ordered but of demands to be attended to and respected, according to the contradictory ways in which they touch and affect each other, or work in harmony and opposition, or resemble and oppose one another. Thinking of the life of the house in these terms, which have little to do with magic or myth in the pejorative sense of such words, enables us to begin to see the limits of the French engineers' provocative technique of order, and the political mythology to which it gives rise.
>
> (Mitchell 1988: 51–2)

CONTEXT AND INTERPRETATION AT EXPO'92

As a world exhibition it is hardly surprising that the Expo'92 generated the kind of representational model Strathern was seeking to combat or at least draw attention to in her critique of the ubiquity of the cultural construct in anthropological accounts. The Expo was clearly located within particular western cultural and political practices, simultaneously creating a semblance of order yet also hyper-aware of itself and of the artifice of its own forms and practices. It is important to appreciate the extent to which the Expo was produced for public consumption and how much of what was going on there was therefore highly accessible. There were press packs, daily bulletins, reams of printed information, videos, postcards, guidebooks, maps and even architects' drawings. There was also a continual running commentary in the national and international media. The Expo world constructed its own external reality to which the public were offered numerous guiding frameworks, to the extent that it was not necessary to go to Seville to find out a great deal about the Expo.

In this sense, the exhibition was in many ways a typical instance of its kind and reproduced many of the forms and intentions of the world fairs of the nineteenth century. The following account of the Franco-British Exhibition held in London's White City in 1908 could have been a description of Seville's Expo'92:

It was a spectacular affair, with opulent pavilions in a mixture of styles, an artificial lake and endless entertainment facilities. Restaurants, fairground rides, sideshows, theatres, shops and a huge sports stadium were interspersed amongst the fine- and decorative-arts buildings, the science and technology halls and the administration blocks. Miniature trains and boats carried people around the site, and the superb gardens echoed to the sounds of orchestras and brass bands playing in the numerous bandstands. Art and science gave the whole a sound pedigree. The Palace of Fine Art in particular attracted comment for four superb displays, of French Art 1200–1800, Modern French Art, British Art 1300–1800 and Modern British Art.

(Greenhalgh 1991: 82)

In many ways the form of the great exhibitions has been maintained despite the changing economic, social and political circumstances. Nation states displayed cultural artefacts and technological expertise in their individual pavilions, seeking to educate and entertain the visiting public.

The obligations of the organizers of a fair with universal status are less concerned with the actual bringing together of exhibitors from all over the globe than with enacting a theme that simultaneously promotes the unity of mankind and the uniqueness of individual societies. The theme for Expo'92 was 'The Age of Discoveries'. The focus of the fair was, as always, human progress and each participating nation competed to produce evidence of its latest scientific and technological developments. Despite the competition the fair also continued to provide the venue for massive displays of transnational solidarity, in which nations collaborated to articulate their common commitment to progress and modernization, in the spirit of friendly competition: 'World fairs built idealized consumer cities within their walls. They presented a sanitized view of the world with no poverty, no war, no social problems and very little nature' (Benedict 1983: 5).

Yet in its late twentieth century guise this universal fair distinguished itself from those of the previous century in the degree to which it was aware of itself, of its own history and its own artifice. The Corte Inglés, an up-market chain of Spanish department stores, marked its presence at the Expo with a children's playground made up of models of architectural icons from previous world fairs; a miniature Statue of Liberty stood alongside a miniature Eiffel Tower which visitors were encouraged to climb in and around. Thus a playful reflection on the historical context of the Expo was visible as part of the on-site entertainment.

The exhibitors mused on the nature of modernity and explicitly addressed the central issues in sociological debates about globalization such as: multiculturalism and the plural nature of society; the links between the global and the local; the temporal and the universal; the ironic play with similarity and difference; the familiar and the strange; the traditional and the modern; uniqueness and wholeness; discontinuity and continuity.[9]

The integrating effects of electronic technologies, global capital and the shared simultaneity of televisual media were addressed in the exhibits. The Expo itself was in many ways constituted through these possibilities. The histories of technological innovation were displayed although not all nations chose to promote the same version of modernity, as will be discussed further in Chapter 4. In the most general terms there was a clear distinction between those nations who sought to display the development of resources, the production of wealth and the promotion of health and education, and those who played with the possibilities of hyper-reality afforded by the most recent innovations in communications technologies and the commodification inherent in capitalism. These distinctions clearly illustrated the tensions between production and consumption as possible foci in contemporary considerations of the nature of modernity.[10]

Familiar questions of identity were also highlighted. Thus while the Expo marketed the nation state, and sought to display national cultures and promote them as commodities to be consumed by tourists and business investors, some exhibitors were also raising quite explicitly the question of 'what is a nation?' The exhibitors provided visitors with contextual information for 'knowing' about the particular nations, they gave information on sources, influences and points of origin, but they did not pretend to be in any way exhaustive.

An explicit guiding principle for many of the national pavilions was the desire to disrupt stereotypes.[11] Peru for example had very little Inca material in an attempt to show that they could trace their history back twenty-seven centuries beyond the Incas. Japan concentrated on tradition rather than technology and Britain took the reverse tactic, working explicitly against an image of an isolationist tradition-bound nation of Beefeaters, Welsh ladies, Scottish kilts and morris dancers. Late twentieth century Britain is the nation constructing the Channel Tunnel, linked to Europe with the latest communications technologies, a vibrant economic force in the contemporary world.

Other challenges to the stereotype were more radical and worked against the concept of the nation altogether. Switzerland for example greeted pavilion visitors with a Ben Vautier artwork from 1935 consisting of the message: 'Switzerland does not exist'. The accompanying explanation pointed out that there was no common culture or language in Switzerland. This starting point of their exhibition, the challenge posed by the lack of a common linguistic and cultural foundation for their national identity, was dealt with in their exhibit which suggested a solution in communicative multiplicity, summed up in the slogan 'je pense donc je suisse'.

Another very radical exhibit was that of Czechoslovakia – a pavilion which housed a glass sculpture displayed through a show of light and sound. Czechoslovakia had removed a Communist government during the planning stages of the Expo and the new organizers held a competition for the design of the interior of the pavilion. This abstract modern sculpture won by nine votes to seven. The judges liked it because they believed that it would produce a memorable experience for those who visited. They thought that the experience of engaging with the exhibit, of using it to explore one's own fantasies and associations, would furnish a more worthwhile memory of the Expo. They said that other displays of culture and history would soon be forgotten. Furthermore they wanted to distance themselves from the content of their recent past. The commissioner with whom I spoke had been on the selection panel and had himself favoured an exhibit which consisted of a space of grass, a flag pole and the Czech flag: no past just a new future.

The Expo, so clearly located within particular western cultural and political practices, thus provided an example of the effects of cultural constructionism associated with a particular form of representational practice. Each pavilion was different and furthermore sought to establish difference by addressing the possible preconceptions of visitors. Each instance was unique and partial, yet engaged in the same debates, reflecting on the same possibilities.[12] The Expo provided a concrete instance of endless replication, a cultural artefact built as if to demonstrate the possibilities and limitations of an entirely consumerist world. Thus there was the appearance of choice, of multiple perspectives, yet the cultural forms on show were nevertheless clearly reformulations and repetitions of each other and of previous events. Sameness and familiarity undermined the promise of difference.[13]

As suggested above it is not just proliferation but also implosion that accompanies the notion of the construct. The exhibition represents the world, provides contexts and connections for an understanding of external realities, but its reflexivity simultaneously confuses or confounds the distinction of insider/outsider, representation and reality. How should we approach the relationship between interpretation and context in an institution which itself reflexively utilizes the techniques and knowledges that social scientists are still grappling to comprehend and transform into metaphorical idioms for the purposes of description? The problem is illustrated by the Siemens exhibit which evoked an image of the relationship between tradition and innovation, in which innovation was shown to be tradition transformed. The point was reinforced by the movement of the auditorium seats which circled around the same spaces whose contents were transformed and recontextualized each time they were reapproached. A recorded commentary declared that transformations in communications technologies had developed until isolated systems reached their limits, then came the most recent transformation, the evolution of networks and the merging of systems. The film that followed, also about the evolution of networks, had a philosophy credit. My sense of anthropology as a rather pale reflection of the cultural idioms of our time was growing. Anthropologists were not the only ones moving from identities to relationships, we were simply using metaphors which had lives and uses well ahead of our appropriation.

The reflexivity of the exhibits was often highly ironic, as in the Irish demonstration that certain forms of rationalization can lead to patent absurdities. Savant Deselby is a mad scientist character who appears in the writings of the comic novelist and satirist Flan O'Brien. The Irish mounted a display of Deselby's investigation into time and eternity which built on the fact that we can measure the time it takes for light to travel to a mirror and back to the eye. Thus when we look at a mirror we see the past. Deselby arranged a series of parallel mirrors and claimed that he saw himself as a beardless, twelve-year-old child. He could not get right back to infancy because of the curvature of the earth's surface. The mirrors can reveal endless instances of a particular image, in this case one imbued with the consciousness of a present divorced from its past but turned back on itself rather than offering a liberation for autonomous actors in the future!

Endless reflexivity has a similar effect on the generation of contexts and interpretations as Deselby's mirrors. But this is not the only problem for the would-be anthropologist of such an event. We have also to deal with its highly textual nature. I have suggested that the Expo is about the public production of image and discourse. In this sense it is perhaps the archetypal form for those cultural theorists who treat culture as text, as construct, as fodder for hermeneutics. Like it or not, the event is textual and vastly over-interpreted. The over-interpretation is part of what constitutes the event. Cultural forms are interpreted quite promiscuously in the promotional literature. Spain and Seville for example operated as both positive and negative icons. On the one hand they stood for marginalization within Europe and evoked the north/south divide, on the other they reminded the world of Spain's centrality to European modernity, owing to its role in discovering America. The interpretative possibilities which this event afforded were reflected in an article from the Iberia in-flight magazine:

> In this electronic age, with the Planet turned into an information network, and in which everything has become instantaneous, Watt's steam engine appears in the Pavilion of Discoveries as a piece of pure archaeology. Its immense legacy included repression as well as benefit, frustration as well as hope. The mushroom cloud which follows nuclear fission is perhaps our guarantee against anything so terrible ever happening again.
>
> (Iberia in-flight magazine)

For the writer of this piece the Expo evoked the failures of modernism and this meaning was then projected on to the exhibition:

> This reflection upon the role and scope of technology gives this Universal Exhibition, if not a pessimistic note, then a note of caution which stems from disappointment. Thus there is a return to pre-industrial materials, with the architect Tadao Ando deciding to use wood for the Japanese Pavilion, as have Chile and Switzerland for theirs.
>
> (Iberia in-flight magazine)

My interpretation differed from that of this writer, as I brought different contextualizing information to bear to produce a less coherent image. Thus I noted that while Switzerland might have endorsed the journalist's interpretation, Japan's position seemed more ambiguous as the Japanese display was complemented by the presence of Fujitsu, sited opposite, and displaying pure technological effect. Chile's exhibit seemed to me to be more concerned to make an assertive marketing statement. Their claim was that they could get anything, anywhere, anytime, even an iceberg to Seville in the middle of summer. The wooden pavilion which encased the iceberg was as likely to have served as insulation as it was to have made a statement against technological progress. Indeed environmentalists protested about the ways in which the Chileans had removed the iceberg from the Antarctic.

In both these interpretations, meaning is attributed to objects as required for the wider argument. Such is the nature of interpretation.

As a textually produced event, it was also impossible not to pre-interpret. Before I went I already knew a lot about the history, politics and economics of this institution and its particular occurrence in Seville. Interpretation was thus an integral and inevitable part of the experience of the Expo. It also entailed contextualization, the bringing to bear of additional information to render things meaningful.

However interpretation was not necessarily the only or even the most appropriate response to the event. How might knowledge or understanding acquired via interaction or situated practice differ from that acquired by contextualization?

My initial response to the Expo site was that overwhelming sense of alienation that I associate with being a tourist, when it is virtually impossible to contextualize what is going on and a feeling that one lacks the cultural 'know-how'. At the Expo there was obviously a huge amount happening but it was very hard to work out what. For example I suddenly came across an Indonesian procession. People lined the walkway to watch and dispersed again when it had passed by. As I might have expected at the start of fieldwork, I didn't know how to interpret although I sensed that I could find out if only I knew how. Then something else happened which grabbed my attention and that of other people, a crowd formed, an event occurred although I was not quite sure what it was, as it passed me by, and then people got on with what they had been doing before. The activity was something I watched, something that was happening outside of me, I did not know where it came from, where it was going to, what it was for or what it was about, it was just there.

It is important to me to record these first impressions because my subsequent understanding of what was happening was one of the ways in which my experience at Expo must have differed from that of many visitors. But I also want to point out that much of my early confusion resulted from my ambition to understand, my desire to engage with the representational paradigms of the Expo exhibit. Such confusion was however neither necessary nor particularly appropriate. I was not required to understand, to grasp the whole, although such a project was presented as a possibility. Experiences were also laid before me for the purpose of enjoyment. In this respect what I had to learn, in order to participate, was how to enjoy. This distinction between understanding and enjoyment is acknowledgedly problematic as many of the possibilities for enjoyment were pre-planned and depended on at least a recognition of the intrinsic inter-textuality of the event and thus on interpretative practice. At the most basic level visitors would have had to recognize the Eiffel Tower and the Statue of Liberty to appreciate the Corte Inglés' children's playground. It is thus not interpretation per se which causes problems but interpretative practice which is directed towards particular domains of contextualization.[14] Contextualization as part of the generation of anthropological knowledge is not the same as the contextualization integral to the experience of visiting and enjoying the activities taking place on the Expo site.

This point will be dealt with further in Chapter 5 which looks at the enjoyment of interpretation. For the purposes of this chapter I want to pursue my interest in the two distinctive kinds of knowledge: knowledge achieved via contextualization and that achieved via interaction.

What did it mean then to do an anthropology of this event? Whose knowledge would I be attempting to approximate/translate? The event was obviously highly complex, but the problem was not simply one of how to handle a multiplicity of perspectives. There was no obvious point of identification through which to produce a generalizable ethnographic subject, which would not simultaneously prevent me from understanding the wider event, but anthropology can handle such situations through an appeal to multiple perspectives, overviews, contested interpretations, etc. The problem was not to do with the complexity or scope of the event but with the challenge it offered to our conceptions of ethnographic knowledge, and my ability to stand outside the event in order to present such knowledge.

Anthropologists normally expect to produce this knowledge through the detailed observation of their relationships with those with whom they are living and working. We look at how people react to us, and at how they react to others in our presence. We seek to identify the various ways in which we might participate in a particular event. Furthermore, because we tend to look at cultural 'others', it is sufficient to understand the relationship between us to know something about how those we study live their relationships. At the Expo I had the problem that my anthropological insights were inherently biased towards the recovery of representational knowledge through contextualization. Expo was designed for rapid consumption, for fleeting visits. People queued for hours to get into most pavilions. Most visitors saw relatively little of the whole and what they did see they tended to see quickly. Working with a press pass I could see more, and see it more easily. I could stay longer, I had a chance to go back and to get different kinds of explanatory materials. Thus the paradox of participant observation became apparent. The distance required for observation confounded the knowledge acquired through participation, for many of my fellow participants were just passing through.

How does this differ from the standard experience of anthropological fieldwork? Traditional ethnographers sit in the village. Their lack of understanding is like that of a child, and through participant observation, simultaneously standing outside and immersing ourselves in activities we do not fully understand, we attempt to catch up on a learning experience. It could be argued, as Clifford has done, that the site of anthropological knowledge is no longer the village or the house, but is the motel or the hotel lobby, a space through which people move (Clifford 1992). His point is that the world is not static and anthropology is having difficulty in maintaining the fiction of a stable context for the social relations we describe. But this image of movement does not quite capture my problem. I became increasingly aware that there was not necessarily any particular knowledge to be recovered in the sense of patiently piecing together the implicit knowledge of those around me. In a very short time, I knew more about what was going on than most visitors, yet at the same time I did not know, and could not find out from sitting there, how the visitors were contextualizing these experiences for themselves. When I asked two British visitors what they thought about the UK pavilion, they said that it was better than the Welsh Garden Festival but not as good as Disney. Their evaluation entailed a contextualization in terms that were not available to me through participant observation.

What does that say about the notion of context that anthropologists implicitly work with? Putting things into their social context implies the attempt to make explicit the connections that are made by people as they live their relations to other people and to things (Strathern 1995). An understanding of the process of contextualization has always implied looking beyond the immediate, available interactions, but we have also maintained that the ability to make or even recognize appropriate connections emerges through the period of extended participant observation, indeed this is the rationale for our extended periods of fieldwork. In a situation such as Expo that is quite patently not the case.[15] The ephemeral presence of the Expo visitors made evident the ways in which anthropologists render experiences comparable through observation.

Furthermore the knowledge produced through interaction either referred me elsewhere or echoed the same lack invoked in me by the representational paradigm. This British couple who were highly suspicious of me approaching them, thinking that I was probably trying to sell them a time-share, basically did a deal to talk with me to swap information. They would tell me what they thought about the British pavilion, if I would tell them what I knew about what was going on and what they should go and see. Thus by studying Expo, by observing, standing back, accumulating information, I was in effect cutting myself off from the experience of many of those around me. This again is an aspect of all ethnographic research.

Experience is interpretative, yet to make anthropological knowledge very particular kinds of interpretation are involved, interpretations which require contextualization in terms of a specific set of theoretical concerns. When those concerns are in fact generated by the wider social conditions in which one lives and works the process can appear very self-referential. In short, by doing anthropology at Expo, by trying to articulate for myself something of they way in which it was operating as a cultural event, by constantly trying to contextualize what I saw and heard, I would inevitably get involved in a kind of grotesque parody of the event itself. For the Expo, as cultural event, played with the idea of context and showed it to be about both accumulating and adding knowledge, enabling links between nations, uniting them in various evolutionary histories from 1492 to 1992 and beyond. It also showed how the effects of this approach to knowledge contribute to the sense of receding horizons, to gaps and uncertainties. So why not simply enjoy? You cannot have it all but you can have choice.

The Expo exhibits were constructed in a quite deliberate

fashion and intended to convey certain meanings. Contextual information was required to interpret these modernist messages and to reveal the processes through which nations and multinationals were or were not successfully produced as viable social entities which could then be brought into relationships. But the contexts were not implicit, they were on display and their display produced a parallel but different set of effects. Culture was everywhere, each nation had some. It appeared in multiple guises, as high art, civilization, history, identity, daily life, evolutionary process. The pluralism was presented as a series of options. Culture, visible as a construct, is simply a matter of choice or image to be consumed, effective if it played into particular emotional responses and provoked pleasure or stimulated desire for further consumption.

In this scenario the cultural constructionism of western representational practice now appears as integral to the embodied knowledge of social actors. The problem for anthropology is that this process undermines both the expertise of academic knowledge and the authenticity of the subjects concerned.

AUTO-ANTHROPOLOGY: CONTEXTUALIZATION AS INTERACTION

There is considerable resistance or scepticism in contemporary anthropology towards a Geertz-style hermeneutics, that kind of thick description that treats cultures as texts which can then be interpreted to reveal meanings (Geertz 1973). How are we to know whose meanings the interpreters produce, and why those meanings at that moment? The textual metaphor also implies that cultural practice is intrinsically representational, that social actors are constantly theorizing and textualizing. Some have argued that this approach simply reproduces western, middle-class, academic practice and is anthropology's most pervasive contemporary ethnocentrism.

I see two principal ways in which anthropologists are currently seeking to prevent the representational model from being applied unthinkingly. The first of these is through the generation of counter-examples drawn from long-term, in-depth fieldwork, often among non- or semi-literate peoples. The second is a theoretical approach which seeks to isolate the universalist assumptions within disciplines such as psychology and biology and critique them through the application of a more general comparative method. In both cases these approaches to anthropology depend upon a belief in degrees of incommensurability, in the idea that the comparisons reveal radical difference, not merely further perspectives. In many ways, as I argued above, this approach does suggest that as anthropologists we have more to learn from non-western peoples than from the study of western institutions. However, writers such as Ingold claim that 'anthropology is not the study by westerners of the non-western "other". For in anthropology we study ourselves' (Ingold 1992: 695). In this formulation it is our common humanity that is stressed: 'we look at others in order to come to an understanding of the human condition, studying with or under those who can act as our guides or tutors by drawing on their practical experience of everyday involvement' (Ingold 1992: 695). There is, I believe, an implicit exclusivity in this approach. What about the millions of people who spend time reading newspapers, watching television, going to the Expo? Who are the 'genuine' subjects at the Expo? Does Ingold's formulation of the anthropological project exclude the journalists, the architects, the designers, the academics, the visitors who live the world as exhibition?

Ingold's programmatic statement for the future of (British) anthropology, was also a call to question the salience of representational models in current practice, and to look instead at how people attend to the world and its affordances. The point is that people do more than simply construct or recover prior representations. This attendance to the world is an intrinsically relational process and one in which culture is continually emergent, since the focus is on effect, and forms embody historical process. If we were to adopt this approach for the study of mass popular culture, it would require attention to how particular relations have effects and become visible at particular times and in particular places.

There are quite specific questions of this kind that we might ask of an event such as the Expo and which I will address in subsequent chapters. How do nation states emerge as distinctive cultural entities in this form of public display? What is the relationship between certain contemporary understandings of culture and technology? There are also the perennial anthropological questions such as how does this institution reproduce itself over time and what is the relationship between change and continuity in this process?

However, as I will show in my discussion of both producers and consumers of the Expo exhibits, once we ask these kinds of question, the study of contemporary western popular culture is bound to bring us back to representation. It is here that I strongly disagree with Ingold's derision of what he calls a 'fashionable and careerist interest in the reflexivity born of literary theory'. Anthropology, in my opinion, has benefited enormously from the sophistication of certain approaches to textual analysis which it is increasingly going to have to draw upon to complement a more traditional attendance to non- representational cultural practice. I am not convinced that careerism made literary theory fashionable but rather a need for textual readings which precisely did not privilege, and thereby remove from the complexity of social relatedness, either the author or the reader, the producers and interpreters of texts.

If anthropology's interest is in knowledge and in conditions of knowing there is no incompatibility in bringing together both the representational practices of many people and the attendance to environmental affordances. Representational practices are one of the ways in which people know their world and a salient mode of interaction.

The Expo can be used to draw out a contrast between concepts of culture, understandings of context and kinds of knowledge that are produced through the interpretive process to help formulate a more useful evaluation of the relationship between knowledge achieved via contextualization and that achieved through inter- action.[16] It is an issue that goes to the heart of the dilemmas of auto-anthropology.

Anthropological knowledge is that achieved via both the prac- tice of participant observation and ethnographic and theoretical contextualization. While acknowledgedly partial and particular it also constitutes a certain claim to expertise which then awaits refutation or confirmation from other experts. However for those involved in cultural practice what really matters are the immedi- ate effects of their actions. They are constantly engaged in relationships and are attending to the consequences of previous interactions. There are constructs and contextual features which participants manage to render salient in the process of social interaction but there is no enduring objectification. The problem with the metaphor of the construct is that it renders this process static.[17] It is for this reason that those ethnographic studies of the processes through which apparently stable forms emerge are so useful.[18]

Strathern (1991a) has emphasized the difficulty of using the concept of perspective (context) once awareness of it is brought into play. When distinct perspectives are set alongside each other, as choices for viewers, we experience the 'multiplier effect of innumerable perspectives', the idea that no context or perspective can ever provide an adequate account. The term 'post-pluralism' acknowledges the recognition that increased diversity entails loss. Analytic attention is thus redirected to the lack which perspective entails rather than the possibilities of totalizing vistas which perspective might have entailed in a pluralist framework. In a post-plural cultural environment, the notions of context and culture thus lose explanatory force and the focus on effects emerges as a more appropriate analytical language.

However, there is a twist. As the Expo study makes clear, it is not just anthropological theory that had become aware of the partial nature of the connections which our concepts of context and culture afford. The social and cultural processes through which these possibilities emerged also generated other cultural forms, such as the Expo itself. Here we find that the kind of 'culture' which is displayed is one that can achieve the effect of highly commensurable difference, a commodified object not far removed from our familiar western social scientific concept of the construct. The notion of the cultural construct is one that celebrates multiplicity, perspectives can always be added and the model is thus highly productive in an environment in which both specificity and connectedness are valued. Expo'92 reveals that the cultural construct is a late twentieth century artefact that can now endlessly reproduce itself, continually opening new perspectives that effectively undermine the possibilities for producing that generalized knowledge of power and interest on which critical scholarship has traditionally depended. It is this dilemma which sustains, even generates concern over the tension between knowledge as representation and knowledge as effect.

Anthropologists are in a position to be most attentive to the cultural specificity of knowledge-generating practices, and it is perhaps a specific anthropological interest (rather than expertise) to consider the effects of representational practice. The problem with focusing on representational practices as one of the ways in which people know their world is the self-evidence of such practices for those of us who write and read. We return to the problem of auto-anthropology and the analysis of cultural practices that carry a reflexive awareness of the model of the cultural construct. What can we do with the perspectives once we have a reflexive awareness of them? Do we stop interpreting or simply add more?

A final example: by 1993, the Expo site had changed. The plan was to turn the larger part of the site, that which housed the majority of the national pavilions, into a technological park, a focus for new business development in the city of Seville. The area which had been occupied by the pavilions of the autonomous communities and the major theme pavilions became an entertainment area, a new leisure business, Cartuja '93. New exhibits were set up, one of them a retrospective of the Expo: Memories of the Expo. This exhibit was striking in that it offered yet another perspective, it 'remembered' by reproducing images of the Expo. There were sound-tracks of voices, references to the queues, the heat, the competition for popularity, the ways in which people exchanged information on where to go and what to do. There were physical relics, sculptures, pictures, fragments of the exhibits, and the top floor was entirely given over to an exhibition of cartoons which were produced during the event, cartoons which had appeared in the local press and had documented the day-to-day political tensions generated by the exhibition: the cleaners' strike, the Australian bar that had been closed down with rumours of financial scandal, the furore generated by the figure of a drunk Cardinal which featured in the carnivalesque street processions.

I agree with Ingold that in many cases it is entirely appropriate to stop interpretation and indeed I have tried to bring out some of the ways in which people visited the Expo to enjoy the spectacle rather than interpret it. But the Expo is a key institution in constituting the world as representation. Umberto Eco was not wrong to refer to the Montreal Expo of 1967 as 'message city' (Eco 1983). It is spectacle, but spectacle offered for interpretation and massively interpreted.

My argument is therefore not for an unreflexive appeal to representation, but for the value in looking at what happens when an institution takes up and runs with the possibilities of treating culture as representation. The comments Strathern made concerning the human genome project (Strathern 1992a) are certainly pertinent here. As an institution, the Expo (as the human genome project) aims at a concrete map, a map in which incommensurability disappears. It advocates an organization of knowledge which aims for totality and which ends up simply generating instances of its own process. However, the Expo took the process one step further because it observed itself and flaunted its self-knowledge, finding ways for the constructs of representational practice to interact in their own right. Nation states and transnational companies advertised their products and capacities at the Expo, generating images that themselves create effects without playing the process back through representational paradigms – an uncomfortable analogy for 'good' anthropological practice.

Chapter 3

The nation state

In the nineteenth century, universal exhibitions displayed 'the conversion of the world to modern capitalist production and exchange, and to the movements of communication and the processes of inspection on which these were thought to depend' (Mitchell 1988: 16). Their project was modernization and the marketing of commodities. In the contemporary world the exhibitions have become sites of promotion for both industrial and post-industrial economies. The nation state has been the central politico-economic and cultural unit through which the exhibitions have produced an image of global community. The dominant model for this crucial entity has been that of the egalitarian community of individuals which, as many writers have noted,[1] is consistently reproduced in western representations of national political systems.

This western concept of the nation depends on those particular understandings of the relationships between parts and wholes, between individuals and society, which constitute the basic premises of European individualism and egalitarian ideology. The model depends upon a metaphor of scale, whereby the larger unit, whether this is taken to be a national or an international community, reproduces the form of its constituent parts. Both part and whole function as self-contained, coherent, bounded entities which are mutual transformations of each other through simple principles of aggregation and disaggregation. These principles of equivalence between social units (individuals, nations, states, etc.) tend to naturalize a particular form of sociality in which each individual unit is deemed to hold a particular identity which can be represented and contrasted with other similar units. Thus, while individual units differ from each other, there is an equivalence in this difference. These units can be conceptualized as either naturally occurring or constructed entities; it makes little difference to the ways in which they are thought to combine to form a more encompassing community. In both cases we find the units defined with reference to precise spatial, temporal and cultural boundaries, which encompass and thus demarcate distinctive but equivalent (and politically equal) social and cultural identities.[2]

Such a model of the nation state was highly visible at Expo'92. The Expo press dossier introduces its section on the international zone in the following terms:

> Of the 171 countries which make up the international community, 109 are present at the Universal Exposition. There are 31 European states, 33 from the Americas – including, for the first time in the history of Expositions all the Iberoamerican countries – 18 Asian countries, 20 from Africa and 7 from Oceania. This high level of participation means that 80% of Humanity is represented at Expo'92.
>
> (Expo Press Dossier: 24)

Nations, states and countries are synonymous in Expo usage and when added together they form an international community which embraces all humanity. At lower levels of inclusion are units such as Europe, the Americas or Oceania, below them the nation states. But whichever level one chooses, it is clear that the main constituents of these universal exhibitions are the named territorial units, each with a specific and demonstrable cultural identity and a particular historical trajectory of emergence. This principle of equivalence also lies at the heart of the modern nation state as a political entity. Modern societies are founded on the contract, elaborated between politically equal individuals, that distinguishes the modern nation state from pre-modern hierarchical social structures in which subjects are linked by relationships of complementarity and subordination.[3]

One of the themes of this chapter is to look at both the possibilities and the problems inherent in this enterprise. Processes of modernization are complex and heterogeneous, modern nation states are not of a kind. My aim is thus to look at the relationship between the principles of modernity and modernization that the concept of the nation state encapsulates, and the concrete manifestations of this form when produced as a particular cultural artefact for public consumption. My suggestion from the start will be that the relationship is highly problematic and that even the controlled environment of a universal exhibition cannot paper over the cracks in this most central of modernist enterprises.

In 1992 the Spanish state tried to demonstrate its ability to mobilize the relevant democratic and bureaucratic mechanisms, which would reveal its status as a modern nation state. The task was daunting: how to produce the image of an ideal form, through the staging of an event which was bound to reveal (i) the historical and cultural specificity of the nation state as a conceptual entity, (ii) the limits of such entities for the organization of contemporary economic and political life, and (iii) the problems in positing cultural equivalence between dissimilar entities?

The first of these problems was implicit in that rationale through which Spain had argued for its right to stage the exhibition in the first place. The year 1492 was produced as a point of origin for Spain's modern national history. However by making such a starting point explicit, and by invoking historical process, the image of the nation state as a timeless and enduring social entity was somewhat undermined. In what sense did the nation state exist in fifteenth century Europe? How was the emergence of the nation state linked to other processes of modernization? What is the relationship between the old European states and the new nations of the twentieth century? The second problem emerges when we look in more detail at how exactly Spain managed to mount the exhibition. It was *non*-national entities, most particularly the supra-national corporations, whose interests generated the financial possibilities for the staging of an event which the Spanish state could quite patently not afford. Panasonic, Rank Xerox, Siemens, IBM and Fuji were among the official suppliers. Spanish banks formed the core of official sponsors together with Coca-Cola (Spain). All these companies contributed a minimum of 1,000 million pesetas in products, services or more direct funding. Finally, the Expo rhetoric in itself was not enough to conceal the discontinuities and heterogeneity which characterized relationships both within and between nation states. Nevertheless, this was the challenge, and it was a challenge for which the universal exhibition could claim a particular track record of expertise and a certain degree of success. For almost 150 years this institution has, despite the odds, furthered the image of the modern nation state as a self-evident and enduring social entity. The following section looks at some of the standard techniques through which this was achieved.

TECHNOLOGIES OF NATIONHOOD

If we think of the nation state as a value (Hannerz 1993) or an imaginary entity (Anderson 1983) that has to be promoted and continually recreated to be sustained as real, then we need to consider the social mechanisms through which this is achieved. The Foucaultian notion of social technology is helpful here. Foucault used the idea of social technologies to refer to the various techniques through which knowledge is produced and naturalized. He looked at the development and deployment of discourses around certain objects of knowledge, and at the ways in which particular institutions engage in processes of naturalization which render constitutive social relations and interests inaccessible or invisible.[4] If we think of technologies as knowledge-producing tools (Shapin and Schaffer 1985), then the universal exhibition provides a rich site for an investigation of the mechanics of fact-making with reference to national cultures and nation states. Furthermore, the idea of the exhibitions as technologies of nationhood also has the appeal of an apt metaphor which invokes those processes of decontextualization and standardization which characterize the relationship between technology and modernity in certain dominant western theories of knowledge.

As Foucault himself has traced,[5] and others have developed,[6] there was a move in the nineteenth century away from naturalistic modes of knowing which concentrated on the similarities or otherwise of the surface features of particular phenomena, to analytical ways of knowing which involved going beyond surface appearances in order to discover principles operating at the level of deep structure. These ways of knowing were developed in the new disciplines of, for example, chemistry, geology, biology, physics, linguistics, etc. They were also fundamental to practical applications of this knowledge, and operated as the conceptual cornerstones of the Industrial Revolution with its reliance on replication and the rationalization of productive processes. The abstraction of principles of organization which could then be reconstituted in standardized relationships of cause and effect both introduced a notion of parity in social processes and simultaneously rendered these processes technological. The rationalizing promise of technological development lay at the heart of modernist ideas about progress. Not only could the unpredictability of social relations apparently be side-stepped but natural processes themselves could be broken down, natural laws discovered and efficiency and control maximized in productive enterprises. To think of the universal exhibition as a technology of nationhood is thus to consider the processes of standardization and particularly the analytical procedures through which social forms are rendered equivalent through the display of particular, apparently defining, component elements.

There are at the universal expositions some very standard techniques of distinguishing nation states through representational practices which simultaneously render them equivalent. For example, in the Official Guide to the Expo, each participating nation presents itself with an image of the flag, the name of the capital city, the population and territorial extension. Each nation has an anthem which was performed to welcome Heads of State and other visiting dignitaries. Some nations, such as Venezuela, had daily ceremonies outside their pavilion when the flag was raised and the anthem played. At this most basic level then, the nation state was produced as a territorial unit with key symbolic identifiers (flags, capital cities, anthems) and a quantifiable citizenship. These symbolic identifiers were most clearly visible on the National Day, allocated to each participant, when official ceremonies, street parades and folkloric performances encouraged the display of national dress and national dance. National culture was also on show in a continual programme of artistic performances (music, dance, opera, theatre, etc.) which ran throughout the six months of the Exposition, each performance clearly identified with its state of origin. Almost all the pavilions contained displays of canonical objects of national pride, works of art and literature, and national industrial products (the United States used Coca-Cola, and several of the African pavilions displayed their own brands of beers and soap powders). Heroic national figures, particularly explorers, scientists, inventors and industrialists,[7] and 'natural' landscapes displayed on film and video were also commonplace and operated simultaneously as examples of technological innovation and enduring cultural heritage. Some nations such as Australia and Brazil produced reconstructions of exotic environments. Chile had brought an iceberg from the Antarctic to serve as the centre-piece of their national exhibit.[8]

These kinds of material representations of national achievements and attributes were the commonplaces of the Expo displays. All the pavilions referred in some way to similar material symbols of the nation and engaged with a notion of culture both as 'particular forms or types of intellectual development'[9] and as an enduring cultural tradition and character. It was only in the degree of association with one or other aspect of these generally recognizable symbolic forms that the pavilions differed. Thus France and Italy for example paid attention to the relationship between artistic cultural production and technological developments. The first room of the French pavilion traced the evolution of knowledge through the development of printing from manuscripts to the printing press to computer-based publishing; technologies that were displayed alongside the canonical books of the French literary tradition. Italy gave considerable space to demonstrating the relationship between culture, communication and memory, starting with an exhibit that centred on the development of new theories for the laws of vision with the emergence of perspective in the fifteenth century, and ending with a display of the ways in which Italians were involved in the most recent innovations of the telecommunications age. The UK, by contrast, was among those who placed more emphasis on an industrial product, (British) steel, as the material which gave coherence both to the structure of the pavilion and the experience of the visitors as they moved through this structure.

In all cases the relationship between contemporary nation states and processes of modernization were quite apparent, as the work of writers such as Gellner (1983) and Anderson (1983) have led us to expect. This close identification of nationalism with modernization, with the 'great transformation from feudalism to capitalism' (Segal and Handler 1992), was itself one of the techniques through which the cultural specificity of the emergence and character of particular nation states has been obscured, and not simply at the Expo'92, but in the social scientific literature more generally.[10] The tension between romanticism and positivism, between images of an enduring past and an innovative future, between the nation as cultural entity and the state as rationalizing bureaucracy, has been central to the image and conceptualization of the nation state at universal exhibitions since 1851. This tension, itself central to current understandings of modernity, is salient in both academic production and political debate, particularly in the oscillations between cultural essentialism and cultural constructivism.[11]

These tensions are embedded in the ways in which nation states emerged in the context of nineteenth century Europe. It is easy to forget that the very particular conflation of political and cultural entities which distinguishes the modern nation state was a recent social phenomenon in the mid-nineteenth century, and one which the cultural complexes of the universal exhibitions were precisely designed to promote, operating as stages for new understandings of national culture.[12] While the concept of the nation as a racial and subsequently a cultural entity has a long history going back at least to Roman times, it was not until the late nineteenth century that the term came to denote both a political entity, 'a state or political body which recognizes a supreme centre of common government', and also 'the territory constituted by that state and its individual inhabitants as a whole' (Hobsbawm 1990: 14). It was this notion of the nation as a coherent and enduring cultural unit that was taken up by the French revolutionaries as they sought to articulate a moral alternative to absolutist monarchy, and it was in this European struggle for rights to political representation and participation that the concept of the nation took on those connotations of the legitimate community which all nationalist movements from the nineteenth century onwards have sought to establish through the material demarcation of sovereign territories (Pearson 1994).

Institutions such as world fairs and national museums thus had a crucial role to play in demonstrating the enduring presence of what were in fact very recent social entities, and in establishing the material traces of an organic development from the cultural nation to the political nation state. This was achieved through the simultaneous appeal to two key paradigms. One the one hand there were those conceptions of community or 'Volk', articulated so clearly in eighteenth century German romanticism, which posited the notion of national character, of a community of people whose shared cultural history imparted a particular spirit to the nation. This spirit was expressed in a nation's particular genius, in its language and cultural production, in what were understood as the external manifestations of essential racial characteristics. The legitimacy of the new nation states depended to a great

extent on the possibilities of demonstrating cultural continuities
with the past, of naturalizing the links between territorial, political
and cultural units. On the other hand, as new political entities,
nation states were themselves icons of progress. They stood as
tangible evidence of a break from previous integrative mechanisms of military force or the traditional authority of social hier-
archy. For the egalitarian nations of western liberalism it was
these new principles of national cultural integration that constituted the modernity of the emergent political entities. However,
the possibilities for conflating the new and the old political entities through an appeal to territorial continuity, afforded precisely
that degree of ambiguity which enabled nation states such as
Britain and France to emerge as paradigmatic examples of this
particular political formation.

Nationalist movements appeal simultaneously to the weight of
tradition and the active construction of a new social consciousness. While this might appear paradoxical (Fox 1990), I will argue
that the paradox is superficial when set alongside the tremendous
generative power of the dichotomies on which it depends. The
relationship between the emergent and the traditional is a key
distinction on which the modernity of the western liberal tradition is founded, a modernity that was built upon the idea of
progress through the scientific establishment (creation/recovery)
of domains of cultural homogeneity and continuity, obscuring in
the process the interdependence of positivism and romanticism.
As Herzfeld (1987: 13) has argued, the rise of empiricism and
the emergence of folklorism at roughly the same time in nineteenth century Europe is no coincidence. Natural and social laws
were naturalized in terms of the same totalizing ideologies that
validated both positivist science and political formations such as
the nation state. Museums and international exhibitions were
crucial venues for the display of the empirical evidence of progressive modernizing national cultures.

Furthermore, many of the recent academic debates on the
subject of nationalism[13] continue to reproduce the very dichotomy
through which their subject of discussion was in fact constituted.
Thus instrumentalists such as Hobsbawm and Ranger (1983)
maintain that traditions are invented; that modern nationalism is
founded on the promotion of artificial constructs, dictated by and
attuned to the pressing needs of a rapidly modernizing society
(Pearson 1994). Anderson (1983) and Gellner (1983), each in

their own way, argue on similar lines that the cultural homogeneity necessary for economic progress in its particular modernist guise, is itself an effect of the early stages of modernization. Thus we see Anderson's imagined communities dependent on the emergence of print capitalism, mass production, and centralized education systems which in turn enable the simultaneous appearance of increased cultural homogeneity, democratic principles of integration among equals and rational free-market economies. Gellner also argues that nationalism, the 'political principle which holds that the political and national unit should be congruent' (Gellner 1983: 1) precedes the nation as political entity; that nation states and national identities sustain the requirements of a modern economy, and that these requirements are based in principles of homogeneity and the spread of particular and specific communications technologies (again particularly standard national languages, printing, mass literacy and mass schooling) (Hobsbawm 1990). These instrumentalist positions can be set against those who argue that modern nation states are built on fundamental and abiding understandings of national identity.[14]

The central point that I want to make here is that while these positions appear to posit two contrasting *temporalities*, one focused on the displacement of tradition by modernity, the other on the continuation of traditional sentiments, it is the conceptualization of *traditional* or pre-modern social arrangements that are not in fact equivalent. The former position, which sets the modern nation state in contrast to pre-modern states, depicts a move from the traditional to the modern as a move away from culturally heterogeneous polities integrated through the imposition of hierarchical principles, to the production of cultural homogeneity through the integration of equals.[15] Alternatively there are those who presuppose a latent parity among subjects founded precisely in that enduring cultural homogeneity which is brought to the fore in the rhetoric of the modern nation state. As Lofgren has pointed out:

> The contrastive technique is found in most identity constructions, but in the nation-building of the nineteenth and twentieth centuries it has a highly central role precisely because it is linked to a belief in comparability and symmetry. . . . [N]ations make themselves culturally similar, all striving to fulfil the new norms for the way a proper nation should be, but at the same

time working hard to establish a distinct profile. As nation
states we are all equal, but as national cultures we should be
as different as possible.

(Lofgren 1993: 166)

Thus we return to the apparent paradox of the central relationship between innovation and tradition in modern nationalist
movements. If, however, we understand the categorical distinction
between modernity and tradition to be itself an effect of modernist discourses and an aspect of identity construction, it is possible
to see how these two apparently contrasting temporalities are in
fact interdependent effects of classificatory techniques by means
of which particular social institutions, in this case nation states,
produced themselves as simultaneously enduring and innovative
(Gupta and Ferguson 1992; Latour 1993). This issue of the interdependence of tradition and modernity in the constitution of the
nation state can best be illustrated by a close examination of
the ways in which particular nations presented themselves, as
discrete and internally coherent entities, at the Expo.

THE NATION STATE AT EXPO'92

Hobsbawm (1990) has pointed out that any attempt to apply the
principles of nationality in a general, indeed universal field, will
simultaneously entail international and domestic political problems and both the place and the time of the Spanish Universal
Exhibition provided somewhat inauspicious contexts for any
ongoing attempt to naturalize the relationship between state and
nation. Europeans in 1992 were particularly aware of the problems and compromises involved in securing the economic integration of the European Community. The break up of the Soviet
Union and fall of the Communist regimes of the 'Eastern Bloc'
presented new challenges to the 'Western nations', particularly
Germany, and the intensity of nationalist wars in the Balkans,
Northern Ireland and the Basque country were echoed by calls
for devolution and the recognition of cultural autonomy in many
other areas. To mention these worlds beyond the universe of
the Expo, is to raise empirical questions about how equivalence
between nation states is produced at such an event when the
nation state itself seems to be such a fragile entity. How do
the ex-eastern bloc nations stand as comparable entities to the

other European nations when the relationship between national economy and national culture, the experience and understanding of modernity has been so different?[16] How are the tensions between Navarran regionalism and Basque nationalism nego- tiated at a universal exhibition which presents them as two com- parable examples of Spanish autonomous communities.[17] How do post-colonial nation states emerge as comparable entities to the old colonial powers? How, in other words, was it possible for the Expo to achieve an image of the nation state as a self-evident, universal, political entity? To answer these questions requires that we look in more detail at how the national pavilions were put together, at who was involved in the promotion of this particular image of the nation state, at the conception and marketing of the contemporary nation state at universal exhibitions.

Expo'92 was officially promoted as a cultural event rather than a trade fair and official statements of objectives produced by Spain, the host nation, emphasized the importance of inter- national accord and the need to build the collective through attention to individual difference:

> Collective aspirations and optimism depend fundamentally on dialogue among nations, mutual understanding, cultural inter- change and the sharing of knowledge. These are precisely the aims of all Universal Exhibitions, and Seville's in particular. They are the keys to entente and world solidarity.
>
> (Expo'92 Official Guide: 13)

These words, attributed to King Juan Carlos of Spain in the opening pages of the Official Guide to the Expo'92 are echoed by the sentiments of the President of the Spanish Government, Felipe González:

> Expo'92 has an important contribution to make in helping us to look beyond this turn-of-the-century period of crisis and reaffirm some of our most basic beliefs. This coming together of people from all quarters of the globe, this display of Man's creativity and his capacity for discovery and invention, and the cultural interchange that all this implies, inspire collective confidence in the future. It represents solidarity among the peoples of the world.
>
> (Expo'92 Official Guide: 14)

And those of Emilio Cassinello, the Expo'92 Commissioner General:

> Expo'92 aims to reflect the universal need for understanding among all its peoples and an awareness that the future of each individual is what constitutes our common destiny.
>
> (Expo'92 Official Guide: 15)

The more particular economic and political aspirations of the hosting nation are played down in these general statements but are referred to in literature directed at Spanish participants, and not only those who might be persuaded to become involved in sponsorship or more general promotion. The following list of aims and objectives is set out in a document produced under the Expo logo by the Municipality of Andalusia and is directed at schoolchildren. In this document the particular objectives of the Sevillian Expo are presented as follows:

1 To serve the interests of the state by showing a new image of Spain and drawing the attention of the international community to Spain's integration in Europe.
2 To strengthen Spain's international links and to emphasize its geopolitical and cultural position as a bridge between continents, nations and cultures.
3 To show the importance of Spanish works in America.
4 To consolidate the Ibero-American Community of Nations.
5 To give space to all nations and companies to pursue their objectives and promote their image.
6 To offer a rich and diverse programme of artistic events both to attract visitors and for transmission by the mass media.
7 To try to stimulate a commitment to the poorer nations and sections of the world.

One key image for the marketing of this event, both at home and abroad, was thus the double significance of 1992 for Spain as a contemporary nation state. The Expo'92 offered Spain the opportunity to reflect on its own modern origins, on the fifth centenary of the 'discovery' of the Americas, that 'turning point in history when man first became aware of his universe',[18] and to contemplate its future in the year in which Spain gained full accession to the European Community.

In terms of the political agenda the Expo'92 had many parallels with the Ibero-American Fair of 1929, also held in the city of

Seville. Conceived at the turn of the century in 1889 as Spain was losing the last of its former colonies, and was beginning to look more like a colonized state itself, this fair was an attempt to establish a new set of trade and diplomatic links with its former colonies. Unfortunately the timing could not have been worse. On the eve of the European depression of the 1930s, Spain was unable to capitalize on this event. Ironically the event was made possible because many of the Latin American economies were experiencing a buoyancy as a direct result of the European crisis. Franco came to power soon after and the 1929 fair in many ways marked the beginning of Spain's long isolation from Europe. The hope for the 1992 exhibition was thus to relaunch this nation for Europe. King Juan Carlos returned to the throne in 1975 and within months had expressed his wish that Spain should host a universal exhibition. Bridges and connections became the central symbols of an exhibition which sought to emphasize continuity with a glorious past and the political and economic capacity for a dynamic future.

This international promotion of Spain's modernity was primarily instantiated in the staging of the event itself, and it was on these terms that government officials worked to gain solid support for the level of economic investment which the overall organization of an event such as the Expo'92 was going to require. Similarly it was in terms of the economic benefits to the region that the Expo was sold to the local Andalusian public. Past connections provided a cultural basis for the event, but it was the provision of new infrastructural links that was going to enable its successful realization: a new airport, a high-speed rail link to Madrid, new motorways, bridges, urban roadways. These developments were presented as beneficial to the whole nation, particularly in terms of expanding employment possibilities and a boost to the regions from which the range of raw materials and expertise would be gathered. Within the city of Seville itself, resources were to be directed to the upgrading and development of luxury tourist accommodation, and the restoration of local Andalusian cultural patrimony. Together these aspects of the project were presented as an opportunity for a more general impulse for the regeneration of the local tourist industry, that aspect of the local economy which itself most crucially depended on the revival of past connections and the provision of future ones. Support for these developments locally was also generated by the knowledge that Andalusia was one of the poorest and more isolated regions of Spain and by an intense rivalry with other urban centres. If Barcelona was going to receive the level of investment required to stage the Olympic Games then the Sevillians did not want to be found wanting in support for the Expo developments. Needless to say the wisdom of these investments was fiercely contested in some quarters. Many people felt that the services and infrastructure which were designed to enable the Expo'92 to take place were not those required to regenerate the Andalusian economy. Fiscal reforms, new employment policies, and long-term financial commitment to social programmes were seen by many as far more important. It was argued that the Expo distracted from these priorities and in many ways exacerbated the deep-seated social inequalities which characterize this region of Spain. In many ways these fears were well founded. The Expo produced hyper-inflation in the urban housing market, cut-backs in public spending on social programmes, and the accumulation of debts which the city and the region will be paying off for decades to come. The new luxury tourist accommodation, forced to decrease prices massively after the end of the Exposition, effectively wiped out whole sectors of the middle and lower end of the market. Those few who already controlled the agricultural commerce of the region have come to enjoy improved facilities through which to conduct their businesses and export their products – but show no signs of extensive local reinvestment. The parallels with the 1929 exhibition are perhaps a little closer than the organizers would admit, and definitely closer than anticipated.

But what of the other nations? What motivated their participation in an act of public relations which might, it could be argued, be equally if not better achieved via other media than the somewhat anachronistic vehicle of the universal exhibition?

In general those who sponsored the construction and running of the national pavilions were looking to promote business and political interests along similar lines to the objectives of Spain itself, tailored to their particular circumstances. For example, the Press Secretary to the British pavilion talked to me about the possibilities that the Expo offered Britain to show a powerful new image to the world: an image of an inventive, creative, original and modern nation. The publications put out by the British Government's Department of Trade and Industry (DTI), looking to promote partnerships between government and private enterprise, stressed the opportunities for British companies 'to demonstrate their commercial strength in the new Europe of 1992 and beyond', and the kinds of opportunities that such collaboration would afford were listed as follows:

The prestige of being involved with a project which intimately concerns and involves the UK Government; the opportunity to build their corporate or brand image; the opportunity to show off products and services from British companies to over 2 million visitors to the UK Pavilion, and to many more through international television coverage; sales leads through contacts with prospective customers; contact with international decision-makers; a highly prestigious opportunity for corporate and trade hospitality with a unique character and appeal; product or service demonstrations; extensive media coverage both in the UK and abroad; and the opportunity to feature the association between the company and the UK Pavilion in advertising and promotional campaigns, and in corporate and sales literature.

(DTI 1992)

The British pavilion was thus offered to business as a marketing opportunity, a focus further underlined in 1988 by Margaret Thatcher's decision to put such exhibitions under the control of the DTI rather than, as previously, the Foreign Office.

By contrast, some nations were looking quite explicitly to attract capital investment for the restructuring of their economies. These messages tended to be confined to the promotional literature while the exhibits themselves were there to attract attention and provide a venue for other negotiations. Both the Czechoslovakian and the Hungarian pavilions offer good examples here. Their corporate sponsors were travel agents, banks and international companies. The exhibits emphasized historical links and particular national contributions to the culture of Europe but much of the literature handed out to visitors simultaneously expressed the sentiment that these links had to be reforged and supported. Past connections and national genius are not sufficient. An ongoing and productive relationship with the European Community would require technical developments for which the Community must take some responsibility.[19] Thus, the Press Secretary for the Hungarian pavilion told me that, for them, the importance of the exhibition was to draw attention to Hungary, to try to establish a sense of their European presence and to promote new economic connections. To these ends the pavilion was used as a venue in which to meet and entertain members of the international business community.

In the most general terms then, nation states and their business sponsors invested in 'image' in a fascinating collaboration which I will return to below.[20] Who ultimately controlled what this image should be varied considerably across the exhibition. In most cases a particular arm of the national government (such as Britain's DTI, Hungary's Department of International Economic Relations or Paraguay's Ministry of Tourism) held primary responsibility and looked for business partners for mutual benefits of promotion and funding. Other nations had considerably less commitment to the event, and had only agreed to attend on the basis that the Expo (as state corporation) would finance their participation. The majority of the African nations participated on this basis and it is significant that these pavilions tended to be run by individual businessmen rather than official government departments. As might be expected there were also local (national) disputes surrounding both the financing of participation and the final image produced.

The Commissioner of the US pavilion explained that the political crisis of the Gulf War had made the funding of the US pavilion extremely problematic. The official institution responsible for the pavilion was the US Information Agency. When the King of Spain had issued the invitation to President Reagan plans had been made enthusiastically and in a mood of optimism. There was a contest for the architect of the pavilion and the Chairman of the US Information Agency had chosen a project, whose estimated construction cost alone was $26 million. However, by this time the President of the USA, the Chairman of the US Information Agency and the Commissioner General of the Expo exhibit had changed, recession had gripped the US economy and the Gulf War had started. In 1990 Congress finally granted $13 million for US Expo participation, the rest was to be raised privately. Not surprisingly, US foreign and economic policies in 1992 were not centred on creating an image for the European Community in Spain. Their exhibit was in fact very low-key, their architecture a bricolage of structures which were to hand in Europe – notably two spherical air raid shelters that had found their way to Germany at the end of the Vietnam War. The centre-piece of the exhibit was the Bill of Rights and a film presenting the inalienable human rights of liberty, life and the pursuit of pleasure. American culture was local culture, represented by over 5,000 performers, chosen from and financed by their local communities. With this background it is not surprising that the US press officials stressed that Expo'92 was not a trade fair. For them the insistence that the Expo was primarily concerned with the promotion of international understanding rather than the marketing of national image was a strategy adopted to deal with the particular circumstances of their participation.

The Russian pavilion was subject to even greater political changes in the course of its elaboration. The huge hangar-like structure, initially planned as a showroom for the technological and military prowess of the Soviet Union, became a somewhat over-extensive exhibit space for diverse Russian cultural artefacts. Exhibits referring to the space programme were set alongside religious and secular art works and small-scale displays of medical and information technologies. Many of the items on display seemed quite idiosyncratic. For example, the model of seventeenth century Tobolsk, the first capital of Siberia, sponsored by the descendants of the last governor of that city who had since lived in Venezuela, was presented to provide a possible link between the promotion of Russian culture and the commemoration of the 'discovery of the New World'. The Tower of Cubio carried the following explanatory label:

> This model is the fictional project of a group of young architects from the old Russian city of Samera. Cubio is an invented city, a dream of an ideal human space where man could live remembering his history and dreaming of perfecting the world. The model of the tower of Cubio is a longing for the architectural culture of the past and an attempt to restore this forgotten culture in Russia. It is based in the traditions of the Russian avant-garde of the 1920s, a time when such architectural discoveries were internationally renowned. It is a conceptual project which tries to achieve, through the philosophy of architectural images, a conceptualization of the complexity and instability of those processes through which our contemporary world emerges.

Back in the Press Office I met a delegation of stony-faced Russian journalists who were scandalized and shamed by the exhibit. The

Press Officer explained to me that they had wanted to see rockets and tanks. He told me how Russia was today a poor nation, which despite the fact that it was having to recover from the effects of dismantling a war economy, was nevertheless still first in many things in the world. He handed me some souvenirs printed for the Soviet exhibit, postcards of war memorials and national military and political heroes, and a wadge of literature about possibilities for investments in Russia.

Taken together these examples illustrate the point that, for many, the overarching rationale for participation in the Expo was the promotion of images which expressed the relationship between their particular nation state and Western European capitalism.[21] This is not simply because this relationship was an area of prime concern for Spain itself. On reflection I would argue that it is in fact a point of continuity with previous exhibitions since their initial conception. If, as has been argued by many writers in this field, the institution of the modern nation state is intimately connected to the development of industrial capitalism, this ongoing connection is to be expected. What has changed, of course, since the mid-nineteenth century, and what continues to change from one universal exhibition to the next, is the field of social relations which constitutes Western European capitalism. In this regard 1992 was a unique event. The nations which chose to participate and the extent to which they attempted to partici-pate with a high profile, was indicative of their commitment to this wider project at this particular historical juncture. Apart from those who did not participate at all, there were many for whom the relationship with Europe, and particularly with Spain, was at that moment relatively unimportant. On the other hand the member states of the European Community all projected them-selves as strong, assertive, autonomous partners engaged in a common enterprise. Alongside these were the many other Euro-pean nations who were engaged in trying to establish a more general awareness of their particular national contributions to the history that has produced economic possibilities for this set of twelve western nations, and who simultaneously sought to pro-mote their national territories, resources and skills as grounds for the continuation and expansion of western prosperity.

In this scenario the relationships between nations are of course fraught with the tensions of political and economic inequalities. The Spanish Government, for example, required the presence of the South American nation states at the Expo'92, as support for the cultural and historical edifice through which it hoped to address it own population and the governments and business concerns of the wider European Community. It required the presence of at least some African nation states to establish the Universal status of the event. The South American and African states in turn could look to find in this event possibilities for investment, for the promotion of tourism, even for the small-scale business activities of particular entrepreneurs who used the pavilions as venues for the sale of artefacts and meals marketed as products of their respective 'national cultures'. Larger companies could use the pavilions as novel sites for corporate entertainment. The ways in which business concerns were able to adopt the nation state as a powerful logo for their own particular marketing strategies will be discussed further in Chapter 4. At this stage I will merely point out that the politicians were also involved in a similar exchange of cultural capital. Heads of state and political leaders used the pavilions as opportunities for their own self-endorsement as national (and thus legitimate) products. Numerous heads of state visited the exhibition, particularly on the occasion of their designated 'National Day'.

The presence of such national political figures also had the effect of obscuring the visibility of the complex corporate sponsorship arrangements through which the pavilions were actually produced and run, and naturalized the continuity of national territory, political entity and cultural whole. For example, the presence of the Prince and Princess of Wales at the British pavilion provided a powerful image of a British territory in Spain, a national culture and economy endorsed and promoted by the Royal Family. As icons of the nation, the presence of the royal couple generated a quite different effect from that of the Chairman of British Steel, the major UK sponsor of this event, or of executives of Eurotunnel, London Docklands Development Corporation, Marks & Spencer or Royal Doulton Limited, the secondary sponsors whose public presence already begins to conjure up the image of far more particular and self-interested concerns. And once we move to the more numerous minor sponsors, their efficacy as public promoters is severely limited by the fact that they might be thought actually to undermine the notion of a sovereign British economy altogether. I am referring here to the many subsidiaries of multinationals involved in the sponsorship of the British pavilion such as Bose (UK) Limited, Coca-Cola Great Britain, Iberia Airlines of Spain and Schweppes Great Britain.

From these few examples it is clear that although the universal exposition does undoubtedly operate as a technology of nationhood, this process through which the image of the nation is achieved is not merely one of homogenization and standardization. It involves a complex alliance of parties who have an interest in producing a sustainable image of the nation state, but it is an image that does not necessarily require the resolution of the state/nation tension. As I will show below, this tension might itself be on display. Thus, what is interesting and what I will go on to look at in the second part of this chapter is that the image of the contemporary nation state does not necessarily require the kinds of culturally homogeneous cultural entities proposed by some theories of nationalism. I will argue that the reasons for this have a lot to do with the relationship between culture and business which the Expo'92 instantiated so well. The remainder of this chapter is concerned with the relationship between the promotion of national cultures and the treatment of multiculturalism within national boundaries. This relationship entails a dynamic interaction between the transnational and multinational entities which will be the focus of attention in Chapter 4.

CULTURAL DIFFERENCE IN THE CONTEMPORARY NATION STATE

One of the more interesting changes which can be seen in the universal exhibitions of the past century concerns the degree to which nation states have been concerned to publicly demonstrate cultural homogeneity. Indeed more generally it has been noted how in recent decades, national cultures are often quite openly presented as heterogeneous and fluid communities. This is not to say that multiculturalism replaces a notion of homogeneity, but that the concepts of sameness and difference are presented as compatible rather than opposed. As Young (1995) has argued, heterogeneity is now the self-conscious identity of modern societies but our new hybrid forms are reformulations of nineteenth century paradigms in which processes of unification and differentiation always did operate simultaneously:

Hybridity shows the connections between the racial categories
of the past and contemporary cultural discourse: it may be used
in different ways, given different inflections and apparently
discrete references, but it always reiterates and reinforces the
dynamics of the same conflictual economy whose tensions and
divisions it re-enacts in its own antithetical structure.

(Young 1995: 27)

Take, for example, the case of Canada:

Canadian officials have declared that Canadian 'multiculturalism' distinguishes their national culture from the assimilationist
American melting pot. Yet despite its apparent denial or rever-
sal of cultural homogeneity, this multiculturalism we would
argue, becomes the homogeneous content of Canadian culture.
In other words, in this ideology, what all Canadians share, and
what distinguishes them from US nationals, is their diverse
cultural heritage. It is only a superficial paradox to say that,
ideologically, diversity makes all Canadians alike. Fundamentally, Canadian multiculturalism reemphasizes the homogeneity
presupposition of modern nationalism, for in this perspective,
the nation remains a bounded collection of individuals who all
differ from one another in uniform and acceptable ways and
who commonly possess the range of difference present in
Canada.

(Segal and Handler 1992: 4)

This easy embrace of the politically anodyne concept of multicultural communities projects a very different approach to cultural difference from that more familiar to the world fairs of
earlier years.

In the great exhibitions of the pre-First World War era, the
importance placed on distinguishing the cultural from the biological as principles of difference was reflected in the varying treatment of human subjects at the fairs. As Segal and Handler (1992)
have noted in terms of a more general discussion of the links
between relations of colonial domination and the rise of European nationalism, populations were mutually constituted as either
'nationed' or 'raced', as possessors of particular cultural attributes
or bearers of racial characteristics. This general paradigm, which
both perpetuated and instantiated the culture/nature dichotomy
of modernist thought, was particularly visible in the traditional

and colonial villages which formed a novel part of the fairs at the turn of the century. For example at the Franco-British Exhibition held in London in 1908, the amusement section of the International and Colonial Exhibition displayed reconstructions of Irish and Scottish villages alongside Dahomeyan, Somali and Senegalese villages (Coombes 1991). While the former were offered as nostalgic images of foundational lifestyles, the historical traditions of European 'nations', the latter were offered as concrete evidence of racial difference:

> The proximity of these 'villages' on site had the effect of accentuating the distance between the European 'primitive' and its colonial counterpart. This was further reinforced by the suggestion in the guidebooks that, even in these supposedly simple European communities, there was evidence of an inherent superiority in relation to the colonized races represented. The predominance of adjectives such as 'healthy', 'beautiful' and 'industrious' together with descriptions of the Irish and Scottish living quarters as 'spacious', compare favourably with the constantly repeated assurances that the Africans are in fact much cleaner than they look.
>
> (Coombes 1991: 206–7)

Rydell's detailed social histories of the US world fairs (1984 and 1993) also stress this close relationship between the emergence of national cultures and the development of colonial empires. The colonizing process was presented as a search for the acquisition of raw materials (natural resources) for the greater (cultural) progress of the 'human race' (citizens of nation states). Thus while raw materials and manufactured products were displayed in the main venues of these early exhibitions, the peoples who inhabited those parts of the world from which these materials were extracted, were displayed in the amusement zones as benchmarks against which to measure the cultural distance of the industrialized nations.[22] Thus while there was a certain incorporation of difference in these early fairs, those who were excluded from the liberal model of an overarching cultural parity of citizens were subject to the imperial discourse of incorporation as property. The contrast with the presentations in 1992 of the multicultural nation state was quite striking and will be illustrated here by a discussion of the exhibits of the European Community and that of Spain.

The European Community: an icon for the multicultural state

Classified by the organizers as an international organization[23] rather than a nation state, the European Community was the one such organization which nevertheless still presented itself in the image of the nation state, with flag, capital city, population figures and territorial extent. This was super-nation rather than supra-nation, providing an umbrella and a low-profile but pervasive rationale for the centrality of other European states at the Spanish Expo. For most Europeans it was not the association with the Americas which made 1992 a significant year, but the emergence of the single European market, the establishment of 'a vast zone without internal frontiers where goods, services, people and capital move as freely *as within one country*'.[24] The Community's aims of a single currency, political union and common foreign and security policies highlight its chosen identity as that of nation state writ large. This nation state is one which embraces the cultural diversity of its constituent nations (in analogous ways to the nationalisms of its member states):

> On the one side, we see a disparate family of nations embracing many differing cultures; on the other, a desire to develop a common identity, to make Europe 'European' – but without succumbing to the colourless uniformity of 'Europeanism' or to the temptation of blindly imitating the past.[25]

Needless to say the multiculturalism referred to here made no reference at all to the presence of non-Community immigrants, guest workers or refugees.

The European Community offered three versions of its presence at the Expo'92. In the first place there were the separate pavilions of the twelve member states, grouped around the Avenue of Europe, with Spain at one end and Great Britain and Germany at the other. The Official Guide is quite explicit about the significance of this presence:

> For the first time at a Universal Exposition, all twelve European Community countries are present in Seville, each with its own Pavilion. The Member States are thus demonstrating their readiness to show themselves to the world as a tangible entity.
> (Expo'92 Official Guide: 229)

The entity was made more tangible by the existence of a separate

Figure 4 The tower of the European Community pavilion
Source: Penelope Harvey

European Community pavilion. The exhibition space of this pavilion was in fact underground, but its visible icon was a 50m tower showing the flags of all the nation states of the Community (Figure 4). Its explicit symbolism was that of a 'large beacon, recalling the message of unity in the diversity of the European Community countries' (Expo'92 Official Guide: 229). Finally there was the Community site, the central space of the Avenue of Europe along which were ranged twelve towers, architectural echoes of the Carthusian monastery which housed the Royal Pavilion, linked by cloth 'sails' which provided shade for visitors, and again symbolized 'the unity and interdependence of the Community countries' (Figure 5). These tangible images of the Community were themselves produced as a collaborative effort between the nation states in the spirit of interdependence, unity and diversity. The Italians had been largely responsible for the infrastructure which was maintained by the Portuguese. The office was run by the French and the Belgians. The architect was German and the interior was designed by the British Company 'Imagination', whose previous briefs had been John Major's Road Show for his electoral campaign in 1992, the Ford Trade Show, the re-launch of the new privatized British Telecom plc, and the promotion of Euro Disney.

The exhibition itself was entitled 'From Renaissance Europe to the renaissance of Europe', and told the story of the 'discovery' of the European Community, via the emergence and collaboration of the Western European nations. The starting point of Renaissance Europe was chosen to coincide with the importance Spain was placing on 1492 as the origin of western modernity. The exhibit drew on techniques of stage design to represent significant themes or events in European history, in deliberate contrast to the high technology communications media used in many other exhibits. The visitor walked through the underground exhibit space through larger than life-size tableaux starting with the great discoveries of the fifteenth century, represented by a huge model of Copernicus at work, and moving on to images of Columbus and the 'great travellers'. The emergence of banking institutions and the printing press, cultural innovations which had definitively shaped the course of European history, was stressed. But similar attention was paid to the centrality of conflict in European history, culminating in the destruction of the Second World War, the urgent need to 'rebuild' Europe and the direct connection with the European Community as the framework for future peaceful co-existence and prosperity.

Figure 5 The Avenue of Europe
Source: Penelope Harvey

The displays made conscious use of visual techniques rather than use of language and the authenticity of the icons was a source of pride to the designers who stressed their validation by historical experts, their fabrication by leading set builders and the enhancement by specially composed music which combined the sounds of fifteenth century viols and harpsichords with those generated by modern electronic synthesizers and samplers. At the end of the tour the visitor was faced by a 98-monitor wall, driven by a computer-based matrix switching system, running from a multi-source laser disc output, which produced 'a unique choreography of contrasting and repeated images of the "Faces of Europe" '.

The intention of the exhibition was to draw attention to the principal goals underlying the Community's foundation:

> [T]o reconcile age-old foes in a peaceful economic endeavour – the Common Market. With this in mind, the exhibition is attempting to show how Europe underwent a major revival during the Renaissance, growing to become one of the most important centres of civilization in the world and continuing its remarkable development in the principal areas of human endeavour [the arts, sciences, technology, trade, the democratically based organization of the State] through to its position at the end of the twentieth century [the European Community presented itself as the world's largest trading power which, together with the United States of America and Japan operates as one of the three pillars of the world economy]; and how, on the other hand, it was constantly torn apart by countless wars, culminating in the last two devastating world conflicts. At the end of this line of development, the creation of the European Community emerges as a source of reconciliation and co-operation by which the countries of Western Europe have radically altered the shape and nature of their relations.[26]

The exhibit ends with a display of the Treaty of Rome and reference to the first European elections. There were displays of the ECU, the Community's common currency, and reams of printed information about EC institutions.

The European Community was thus present at the Expo as a classic example of the western egalitarian nation state, an image which other nations, notably Spain, also used in their self-presentations for global effect.

Spain: the multiculturalism of a European heartland

As host nation Spain appeared in many guises at the exhibition. Spain's European presence was emphasized by the position of its main pavilion at the head of the Avenue of Europe, a location from which Spain was also linked both to its former colonies and to its disaggregated component parts, the autonomous communities ranged around the Lake of Spain. Expo'92, as a state company, was also responsible for the theme pavilions.[27] Thus while the Spanish pavilion picked up very strongly on the idea of a particular national genius and mission in the world, Spain was also present at the exhibition as a global force, an international community and a multicultural nation with a transnational culture. The catch-phrase used to sum up its endeavour in the Official Guide was 'Spain, waiting to be discovered' and the principal themes were given as tradition and modernity, the union of cultures, history and language.

The Spanish pavilion itself was comprised of three separate venues, dedicated to telling the story of how Spain emerged as a nation. Taken together these venues embraced both the possibility of looking back at a history of cultural continuity and cultural (artistic) achievement, and also the forward-looking impulse of scientific and technical expertise which, while starting in 1492, was presented as an ongoing aspect of Spanish national identity today. The classical tradition was represented by an art exhibit, a venue filled with 'universal treasures which reflect the extent of Spain's extraordinary cultural heritage'. Then there was what was in spatial terms the main exhibition space, six halls, with audio-visual displays which aimed to give visitors an overall picture of Spain, a demonstration of the geographical and human variety, the diverse landscapes and climates of the national territory. National history centred on this national territory as the meeting point of different cultures, referring to the Christian, Muslim and Jewish axis and to the impact of the discovery of America on fifteenth century Europe. The central audio-visual was a film, *Caminos del Viento* (Pathways of the Wind) in which Spanish history was presented through the images of a seed blown through time and space. The history of this nation was portrayed as a linear progression from prehistoric times, evoked by traces found in caves and depicted in rock paintings, through the pre-Roman and Roman periods, to that point in 1492 when the meeting of the 'Three Medieval Cultures' reached its apogee. The roots of contemporary Spain were forged at that moment. Christian heritage was presented as the source of contemporary language, law, physiognomy and culture, while the Arab past was more closely associated with what could have been presented as scientific foundations but which actually came over more randomly as the basis of numbers, chess, irrigation systems and 'classical knowledges'. The Jewish heritage was similarly stereotypical, a liberal tradition of urban business. These three forces were said to have existed in equilibrium until the fifteenth century when the Christian aspects came to dominate. Then the narrative moved on to the encounter between two continents which led to transformations in diet and in ideas about nature and the expansion of conceptual possibilities as increased knowledge of the universe, of stars and space, changed the scale of human consciousness. The other crucial theme of this exhibit was the importance of language and communications. The history of the world was depicted as the history of communications technologies and it was in this framework that the importance of the Spanish language was affirmed. Codified in a written grammar in 1492, Spanish was heralded as one of the most widely spoken languages of the late twentieth century, again building bridges, linking continents, a language of the future as well as of the past.

Finally, the most popular of the venues of the Spanish pavilion was their Moviemax production presented in a cinema equipped with a spherical projection system and seating which moved synchronically with the images, intended to make the audience feel 'the excitement of actually experiencing the beauty and attractions of Spain at first-hand'. These attractions were based in the landscape of the nation, but now were somewhat anonymous, the focus having moved to the kinds of physical sensation that any particular image might produce – hang-gliding, riding white waters, travelling on horseback. The idea was to evoke in visitors the emotion of living in the Spanish countryside.

As I have suggested, Spain, more than any other nation at the Expo, took 1492 as an important point of origin for the Spanish nation. For them 1492 was a significant moment of integration symbolized by the expulsion of both the Jews and the Moors and the formation by Ferdinand and Isabella of a Christian Spanish state. Historically multiculturalism worked against the integrity of the nation and the Jewish and Arab cultural foundations appear as influences, visible as traces in the subsequent history of the Spanish nation, their integration facilitated by their subordination to the political control of the Christian monarchs. Contemporary multiculturalism, as represented by the presence of the pavilions of the autonomous communities, is a subdivision of the nation of an altogether different kind. Here the elements of the whole are produced, constitutive parts each with its particular history, economic activity, even languages and customs, but with no overlap of territory or interest. These are the constituent nations of which the larger nation is formed and their presence is yet another statement of the way in which Spain as nation state operates as a facilitator, a cultural mediator and a force for integration and political co-operation, building collectivities through paying attention to individuals, a fine instantiation of the liberal project! Just as there is no tension in being simultaneously British, German, French, etc. and being European, so in the idealized Expo world there are no tensions involved in being simultaneously Basque or Catalan and being Spanish. The state is simply the integrative possibility or structure for the rational realization of collective enterprises. Again this model is a clear example of the philosophy of egalitarian nationalism described by Kapferer:

> Society in the egalitarian view may be likened to a succession of Chinese boxes, each social category, group or unit of organization more inclusive than the one before. The individual is the basic starting point from which successively larger units of ordering are built up.
>
> (Kapferer 1988: 15)

The salience of the individual in this model is crucial, for the principles that sustain national identity and unity in this model are those of contrast, competition, opposition, even conflict.

However, for this model to be sustained, the *nature* of difference is of central importance. While surface differences may be tolerated, even actively promoted, deeper, ontological differences are suppressed and excluded (Kapferer 1988: 215). Stolcke (1995) makes this point powerfully in the contrasts she draws between the internal multiculturalism of the European Community and extra-Community differences evoked by the presence of 'guest workers', migrants, refugees, etc. It is therefore of the utmost importance to note that the egalitarian principle distinguishes

between kinds of difference. There is the difference that identifies
those to be associated, illustrated here by the cases of the European Community and the Spanish presentation of multiculturalism, and the differences that are repressed, removed from sight,
rendered invisible for the damage they would cause to the integrated product, the nation state. In this regard it is interesting to
note how the cultural differences which had to be removed from
sight in this way in the fifteenth century to enable the emergence
of Spain, as a Christian nation state, are now brought back as
foundational differences, evidence of a rich cultural heritage in
which the particular cultural specificity of the contemporary Spanish nation is represented as the direct product of a merging
of diverse cultural forms five centuries ago. The presentation is
particularly ironic when placed alongside the national histories of
the Spanish-American colonies whose specificity is often presented in terms of their mixed origins. These processes of *mesti-
saje* are contrasted to the imaginary homogeneity of the older
founding Spanish cultural forms.

The pervasive multiculturalism of equivalent but discrete entities existed at the Expo alongside a marked preoccupation to
counter those stereotypes of national character and culture, which
might prevent visitors from appreciating the particularity which
participants wished to stress in their exhibits. The concept of the
stereotype is derived from the printing industry, in which the term
applied to the metal plates 'which could be used again and again
for thousands of impressions, without needing to be replaced'
(McDonald 1993: 220). By metaphorical extension, Lippman, an
American journalist, used the term to refer to inaccurate representations, particularly those acquired other than through direct
experience. Stereotyping was seen by national participants at the
Expo as a form of decontextualization in which the specificity of
the relationships within and between national units was achieved
through the distinctions of partial accounts. And of course the
participants were right to be concerned in this regard for while
egalitarian identities are constructed in frames of contrast, the
contrasts themselves are simultaneously projected by others. The
process is dynamic, and there is competition over images and
their associated values. Furthermore the images are themselves
limited, as they are still tied to the possibilities afforded by the
contrasting values of enlightenment, rationality and romanticism.
McDonald has noted that nineteenth century essentialist under-

standings of national character were often expressed in terms of the contrasting values of reason/emotion, logic/intuition, intellect/ passion, etc. Discontinuities between nations were depicted in ways that stressed 'naturality and irrationality dancing on the fringes of rationality and nations alike' (McDonald 1993: 226). The British pavilion provides a key example of the effects of this process at the Expo'92 and shows how the concern to fight stereotypes is a further manifestation of the ways in which national exhibitors were attempting to negotiate the ambivalent relationship between nation and state, between tradition and progress, between singularity and the decontextualizing effects of standardization.

The United Kingdom: fighting against stereotypical associations of state and nation

The tour around the pavilion of the United Kingdom was designed to evoke an exploration of 'original Britain in partnership with the world'. This stress on innovation and an outward orientation was itself presented as a discovery for those visitors who might previously have had a sense of Britain as a tradition-bound, insular state. This theme was addressed quite explicitly from the very beginning of the tour. The guides, referred to as navigators, welcomed the public into the first venue of the pavilion, a room with banked television screens showing images of daily life, ordinary British people going about their daily business, 'a friendly hello from some of the fifty-seven million UK residents'. Before these images were shown the navigators quizzed the visitors on what they knew about Britain in a deliberate attempt to elicit a particular set of stereotypes – of an isolated, unemotional, tradition-bound people who drink tea and sherry, have no social life or social skills and permanently complain of bad weather. The navigators themselves were to present the first challenge to this image. They were young, friendly, outgoing and all proficient in at least two languages.

The issue of multiculturalism was also left implicit in this drive to present the nation as forward looking, not dwelling on the historical past. The image the organizers wanted to project was of a unified democratic nation whose scientific and technological expertise was of use to the wider global community, where connections and communication are more important than origins and particularities. The Press Officer stressed to me that there had been a conscious decision not to divide Britain up into the nations of England, Scotland, Wales and Ireland, but rather to present the identity of a United Kingdom. Instead of Beefeaters and thatched cottages they wanted to look at how Britain was responding to global issues, particularly the challenges of world ecology. The pavilion actively promoted an image of ecological consciousness. The structure was of steel and water. The steel captured the heat and changed it to solar energy which was used to drive the water pumps that generated a wall of water along the façade of the building, which in turn functioned not simply as ornament but as an effective form of air conditioning. The central exhibit area was relatively limited and sparsely furnished by comparison with other pavilions, but the theme was still that of the world environment: fire, air, water and wind, and displays of how British scientists have engaged with these four elements to help solve world problems.

The particularity of the British was thus not presented in terms of a specific continuity of content or form, such as might be represented in the heritage genre which the organizers sought to avoid, but rather in a combination of aptitude and attitude through which equality and difference could be presented as a mediation of the particular (the skills and knowledge of named individuals) and the universal (the general applications of these skills and knowledges). To be British in these terms required no reference to ethnicity or race, to class, gender or age. The spirit of the nation was presented as the activities of free and equal individuals working creatively in ways that the state could direct towards common transnational interests. In this version of the modern nation state (adopted with great enthusiasm by the Thatcher Government), the relationship between state and nation should be no more than a possibility for enhancing the relationship between such individual enterprise and its more general application. On one level it could be argued that such an exhibit substantially changes the kind of relationship between parts and wholes demonstrated by the focus on multiculturalism in the exhibits of the European Community and of Spain. At the UK pavilion there was no focus on the relationship between nation and state, individual and society, smaller constituent units and the encompassing whole. And this was because, as Thatcher herself most famously spelt out, the concept of society becomes theoretically obsolete in such a model, as do all collectivities, be they nations, states, or larger entities such as the European Community. Difference, however, remains important, but as a value, as the possibility for the distinctions that make individual products or persons visible and viable as such.

However, needless to say, this particular presentation of the nation state where both state and nation are rendered invisible was a somewhat fragile artefact. The pavilion shop was probably the most graphic example of this. The Department of Trade and Industry (DTI) had granted the concession for the shop to private business entrepreneurs who, nevertheless, made their business plans on the basis of DTI figures. Among these, for example, was a projection that about 45 per cent of customers would be British. Books and magazines were thus mainly supplied in English. In the event, the majority of those who visited the Expo, and the pavilion, were local Spaniards, and only about 1–2 per cent of visitors were British. Sales were disastrous and by August the liquidators had been instructed to dismantle the shop, which was duly packed up, thereby producing a somewhat alternative, and of course unplanned display in the huge open-plan exhibit space.[28] Critics attributed the business failure to an excess of state control and a lack of information on the cultural profile of prospective consumers!

The British exhibitors had reduced the reference to state and nation to a minimum in their exhibit. The flag was the most salient national symbol, the backdrop to the cascading water that formed the front of the pavilion (Figure 6). The notion of a national spirit was evoked but in a very abstract fashion, and although multiculturalism was also present as a value it was so only when the anthropologist explicitly quizzed the Press Officer. There is no doubt that such an exhibit relied heavily on an established international image of national cohesion which could then be challenged in the performative strategy of evoking and confounding the stereotype. The more enduring ways in which state and nation are conflated in the projection of British national identity, the particular history of empire, the significance of an insular territory in the consolidation of a sense of national bound-aries during the upheavals of the two world wars, and the evo-cation of these principles in the reticence and distrust towards the 'continentals' in the formation of the European Community, are strong enough to need no mention. In this sense the UK

Figure 6 The model for the British pavilion
Source: Department of Trade and Industry

exhibit produced an archetypal image of the nation state: the relationship between state and nation was assumed and not displayed, the will of the individual was a will for co-operation. The formalization of collectivities was rendered irrelevant, even damaging, and diversity was both inherent and productive. What the three preceding examples have in common, however, is that the state was consistently presented as an institution which furthers the interests of the nation and enables the expression of national culture. This was not the only perspective on the relationship between state and nation at the Expo.

Hungary and Czechoslovakia: problematizing the link between state and nation

Hungary and Czechoslovakia were two of the European nations which had, since their acceptance of the invitation to participate in the Expo'92, experienced radical political change in the 'velvet revolutions' of 1989–90. As satellite states of the Soviet Union, there had been no expectation of the conflation between state and nation which West European nation states sought to achieve in the public promotion of national culture. Indeed, as Verdery has argued in the case of Romania, the nation was a focus for resistance and antagonism towards the state, whose authority was quite openly based on the military and economic power of the Soviet Union.

Thus, unlike the twelve nations of the European Community, whose status as 'nation states' was taken to be relatively self-evident and whose exhibits were dedicated to displays which drew attention to their particular national contributions to world cultural progress, Czechoslovakia and Hungary had to find a space in their exhibits to define their contemporary status in contrast to both their own recent past as modern socialist states and their more distant national, but pre-modern social organization. They could not assume an implicit organic development from nation to nation state. Historical discontinuity on the political front had to be balanced with a sense of historical continuity on the cultural front. How was this achieved? How were these 'new nations' distinguished from their former selves and both distinguished from yet rendered equivalent to the core nation states of the exhibition?

Figure 7 The Hungarian pavilion
Source: Penelope Harvey

The tension between a romantic ideal of an enduring past, manifest in the spirit of the people and an innovative future, aided by the rationalizing bureaucracy of the state, was indeed evoked, although as we shall see the effort in both cases was to establish a new link between state and nation and to stress that the principal innovation which they sought to display at the Expo was the novel opportunity to embrace the principles of liberal democracy. This focus also involved a very particular treatment of the past so as to present both a radical break from recent state practice and the enduring presence of a nation or nations which had finally achieved the possibility of self-expression in the domain of public state culture.

The most striking similarity between the two pavilions was that both used single art works to represent the past and future of their nations. The Hungarian display was the architectural structure of the pavilion itself, a building resonant with symbolism explained in the guided tour and the accompanying brochure (Figure 7). The publicity literature declared: 'This pavilion is not an exhibit hall, but rather a work of art with free-standing significance'. Indeed the architect, Imre Makovecz, only accepted the commission on the understanding that there would be no industrial products on display. Modernity would have to reveal itself in other ways. The structure was promoted as an organic form, built from natural base materials, of wood, glass, brick and slate and using traditional handicraft techniques. Its most central symbolic content referred to fifteenth century Hungary:

> The symbolism of the pavilion, and the tour through which the visitor is guided, is the history of Hungary, the history of a frontier nation whose destiny has been to define the barriers between East and West and who finally despite its best efforts was incorporated into Eastern Europe.
>
> (Expo'92 Hungarian pavilion publicity literature)

Thus, in this account of fifteenth century European history, while Spain was involved in the 'discovery' of America, the Hungarians were defending Europe from the Turks, defending Christianity, enabling the development of the western economies in ways which were subsequently to be forgotten. After the Hungarian defeat of the Turks in 1496 the Pope ordered church bells to be rung throughout Europe and this scenario is evoked by the seven bell towers of the pavilion, reminiscent of traditional

Hungarian churches. Passing along a corridor which signified the divisions between East and West that have themselves constituted Hungarian history, the visitor was faced by the only object in the pavilion, a tree with its roots visibly spread out under a glass floor:

> The tree is a universally valid, ancient symbol: light and darkness, depth and height, life, growth, an expression of immortality.[29] The music accompanies us to the bottom of the towers then the bells toll and the doors that have been tightly closed until now open up, and we can cross through them to the other side.
>
> (Expo'92 Hungarian pavilion publicity literature)

The gap between East and West thus bridged, the public could then watch two videos, one on Hungary's twentieth century history, the other a travel film showing images of Hungarian rural and urban landscapes and scenes from daily life.

The theme of discovery was presented in a very interpersonal sense. The participation of visitors in the exhibit was all-important, and the tour was likened to a twenty minute drama. The Commissioner's opening statement in the pavilion guide reads:

> I would like our exhibit to be a surprise for you! A surprise, because you did not know us in this way, and a discovery, because you had not previously had the opportunity to meet with us. I would like the short time you spend in our pavilion to be filled with an intimate mood, close to one another, relating to one another.
>
> (Expo'92 Hungarian pavilion guide)

Czechoslovakia also looked to the past for architectural inspiration, this time to the architectural style of the prewar period, functional, simple and straightforward, 'a way of thinking and a civic attitude, with important democratic content'. The notion of democracy was central to this exhibit. The pavilion contained a large, abstract glass sculpture, displayed through a show of light and sound. There was no guide, no directions for visitors to follow. A roomful of people entered via an escalator every fifteen minutes or so. There was no seating and no indication of position from which to observe the sculpture, which went around three sides of the exhibition space. The music and light show began and when it ended an exit door opened for people to leave. The importance of glass as the key symbol of the exhibit was not stressed in the performance, but was discussed in additional literature which was available but not thrust on visitors. This literature placed more stress on the history of Czechoslovakia, and the need for capital investment if the renovation of democratic traditions was to be maintained. As with Hungary, 1492 was pinpointed as a bad time for Central Europe. While Western Europe was getting richer, Central Europe was losing its economic capacity, diminished in part by the wars which had protected Western Europe from its eastern enemies. The glass was taken as a point of continuity across these troubled times. It is a material which the Czechs themselves produce (in contrast to most of their industries which involve the processing of imported products), and thus displays a certain specificity; it is transparent and could thus indicate a contrast with the previous regime. Here there was to be no pretence or hiding; the glass was also to evoke 'the purity and clarity of our path to the future'; glass-making was presented not simply as an old tradition, but a prosperous contemporary industry with many brands and world markets. The appeal in this pavilion to modernity as a particular form of integration, one which espoused humanist values and principles of egalitarian difference and free choice rather than particular productive technologies, was more explicit than in the Hungarian case. The literature made it clear that the contemporary Czechoslovak position is that the Communist regimes had invested in the wrong kind of modernism, a modernism which brought about over-investment in heavy industry to the detriment of the environment and the human community, as had occurred in fascist Germany and totalitarian Spain. Progress, they stressed, cannot be measured in terms of utility, but through the development of the human spirit:

> The greatest human discovery is not an object of utility but rather the capacity to perceive, to grasp and to experience together. The capability of the human genius is to break the barrier of the rational world of pure technical perfection and enter into the world of dreams.
> (Expo'92 Czech pavilion publicity literature)

This sentiment guided the explanations of the exhibit. The discoveries to be experienced in this pavilion were those that took place in the minds of visitors. Again it is interesting to see the double message which a pavilion such as this produced. On the one hand we have a new, emergent modern nation state, looking for the development of links with western capitalism, asserting equivalence through historically established demonstrations of national genius and the contemporary democratic principles that bring state and nation into a fully co-ordinated relationship. This relationship was quite explicitly discussed in the case of Czechoslovakia, which presented itself as a state with two nations (Czechs and Slovaks) and three countries (Bohemia, Moravia and Eslovaquia). The state embodied the principles of integration and a democratic, civil society which was lawful, humane with a market economy and programmes of privatization to open the country to foreign investment. However, the interesting point is that the territorial and sovereign integrity of the state is thus undermined in the moment of its assertion, a point which seemed to be stressed by an editorial signed by the President of the Czech and Slovak Federal Republic. He wrote against the notion of a personal, selfish state and the ways in which national interests prevail over truly common and global interests. The value he sought to promote in his editorial was responsibility, particularly the responsibility of intellectuals in the dissemination of cultural values:

> [W]e still do not know how to place morals above politics, science and economics. We are still unable to understand that the only real backbone of all our actions – if they are to be moral – is responsibility. Responsibility towards something higher than my family, my country, my enterprise, my welfare. Responsibility towards the order of existence in which all our actions are indelibly inscribed and where they are judged for the first time and justly. . . . If the hope of the world lies in the sphere of human consciousness, then it is more than understandable that the intellectuals just cannot endlessly avoid their share of responsibility for the world and conceal their dislike of politics under the alleged need to be independent. It is easy to have independence in one's programme and leave it to others to realize it. If everyone thought that way, before long no one would be independent. . . .
>
> (Expo'92 Czech pavilion guide)

The importance placed on the role of the intellectual in preserving life itself, brings me to my final and most striking example of the ways in which the archetypal western nation state, the individualist, egalitarian model was explicitly present as an object of contemplation at the exhibition, not taken for granted but publicly questioned.

Switzerland: the nation/state deconstructed

The Best of the Expo, an independent guide to the exhibition, introduces the visitor to the Swiss pavilion in the following way:

> The Swiss have taken a risk. This country of 6.5 million is attempting to show the off-beat side of Switzerland through its art. They may have gone too far. From the towering paper column which glows in the dark, to the unusual exhibits and finally to the *pièce de résistance*, the restaurant, visitors are confronted by oddities. Do they succeed in convincing you there is another side to Switzerland? You decide.
>
> (The Best of the Expo: 96)

The Swiss pavilion not only vaunted cultural heterogeneity, but it went further through a deliberate use of irony and reflexivity to suggest that the integrity of the nation state is somewhat irrelevant in the late twentieth century. This statement was made in the context of a pavilion which was nevertheless bounded, fixed and aiming to display the 'typically Swiss'. The difference from some of the pavilions described above is that the Swiss watched themselves producing this image, and reflected upon that process. For a start the structure was intrinsically temporary and the theme of transience was emphasized. The wooden structure with its paper tower played into widespread themes of the need for environmental conservation, as it was entirely recyclable, and was in fact in danger of falling apart before the end of the exhibition as the paper was not able to totally withstand heavy rain storms. The paper tower was explicitly presented as pure symbol, it could not be visited or climbed, it fulfilled no purpose other than to catch the eye and engage people's thoughts. This theme of impermanence and deconstruction was echoed in the artwork that was the décor of the restaurant. A glass floor revealed the debris of a local bar, screwed up papers and bits of half-eaten food and discarded eating utensils, complemented by a set of 'eaten by' food settings which hung from the ceiling.

Important historical figures had left their traces in the remnants of their meals.

In the main space of the exhibition hall, the issue of national culture was also treated with similar deconstructive irony: 'Instead of Swiss cheese, Swiss chocolate, Swiss herdsmen, Swiss mountains, Swiss precision, Swiss banks: Swiss culture!'. Swiss culture, equivalent to other artefacts, persons, skills, institutions, was introduced through the work of twelve artists whose works of art constituted a sense not only of heterogeneity but also of process, as some of these works were themselves performative. By this means culture was revealed as an elusive, even ephemeral, entity. 'We soon discover that a Swiss culture as homogeneous as this term implies, does not in fact exist.' The identity of the artists themselves was questioned as it was acknowledged they did not all live and work in Switzerland. It was acknowledged that diaspora exist because many feel the need to move away from the narrow confines of places of origin. Swiss artists work abroad, artists from other countries work in Switzerland, Swiss culture cannot be located in a bounded territory. And where that territory was evoked, as a bounded political unit, it was the heterogeneity of the inhabitants that was brought to the fore.

One of the artworks was a musical installation by the composer Pierre Marietan, born in the canton of Valais but now living in Paris. He worked with the idea that Switzerland is 'the nation with the largest number of linguistic dialects in Europe' and took ninety-six voices, each in a different dialect, to produce a 'musical fresco, a composition combining speech and music, as a means of providing a sound pattern of our country'. The work of Ben Vautier, born in Naples and living in Nice, summed up for me the spirit of this pavilion. His connection to Switzerland the nation was as the great grandson of a Swiss painter. His work is described thus in the exhibition brochure (a newspaper of course – transient, mundane, ecological):

> For him there are no taboos. He even disposes of nations, rearranging the world according to ethnic viewpoints. He informs the Swiss, for example, in one of his pictures, that Switzerland does not exist ('La Suisse n'existe pas'). The French-speaking part of Switzerland goes to France, of course, the German-speaking region to Germany, northern Ticino and Grisons to Ratien, and the remainder of Ticino to Italy. But

not to worry: practically every country suffers the same fate! And at least he has some words of consolation for us: 'Je pense donc je suisse'.

Despite a more radical self-consciousness, the Swiss pavilion was in many ways following a very similar agenda to that of pavilions discussed above. Here we find, for example, an attempt to counter stereotypes which were simultaneously subtly reinforced through their negation. Furthermore there were certain aides-mémoires. At the exit to the pavilion there was a small shop where Swiss chocolates, watches and clocks were on sale. The products became more archetypally Swiss in the face of the blatant challenge to this notion in the rest of the pavilion. And archetypal Switzerland was also represented in the main exhibition spaces. There was reference to the Alpine landscape and to the salience of the multiculturalism of the nation state. There was also great importance placed on the notion of expressive freedom, of the problems of conservative traditions which fetter the human spirit. A free press raises questions and these questions are posed openly by the exhibitors. 'Can Switzerland accustom itself to Europe or Europe get used to Switzerland?' 'Can our laws become obsolete?' 'Is tradition more than comfort?' – they even drew attention to the following comment by Woody Allen: 'I believe in the intelligence of the universe, with the exception of a few Swiss cantons'. However, the Swiss pavilion did feel risky. It seemed to undermine the possibilities for its own autonomous participation. It instantiated the receding horizons of identity which deconstructive postmodernism has inflicted on so many political projects which depended on the identification and organization of particular communities or interest groups. With far more irony, the Swiss pavilion made quite explicit what the UK exhibit invoked, namely the fact that there is an awareness of nationalism in contemporary Europe that diverges from that of the integrational cultural objectification of the nation state, and moves towards an image of the nation as the product of individual interests and expressive capacities. My suggestion, as a bridge to the next chapter, is that in such exhibits we can see that nation states are not simply products of international politics, as the historical exhibits of many nations might lead us to expect, but are also the products of a cultural propensity to hyper-individualism and to the economy of multinational capitalism which supports such values.

In this scenario the contemporary nation state no longer requires either cultural homogeneity or territorial integrity. But what challenge does this stance entail? These ideas can be quite easily incorporated into the previous model of the nation state, and indeed at the Expo they exist happily side by side, unremarkable and unproblematic companions. The key to such integration, which is perhaps most succinctly summed up in Ben Vautier's slogan 'je pense donc je suisse', lies in the fact that we are dealing with communities of like individuals, even where these individuals can no longer be confined to bounded territories. The Swiss are alike in their creative response to the deterritorialization of Swiss culture.

As Grossberg remarked, the global postmodern has no proper dialectic. It pluralizes and deconstructs itself, yet it originates in the West, and thus constructs a form of homogenization through difference.[30]

THE GLOBALIZATION OF THE NATION STATE

I have suggested that universal exhibitions have been involved in the global extension of a particular model of the egalitarian nation state, built around the notion of the autonomous, coherent, self-determining individual and an operational tension between continuity and change. In the debates over the development of the nation state this tension emerges in the manifest ambivalence of the relationship between nation and state, an ambivalence which has been taken up recently by various commentators who argue that in the late twentieth century such ambiguities have become so apparent that the nation state is no longer a viable political entity, and certainly not an institution that can be projected with any optimism into the twenty-first century.

The promotion of an evolutionary model from cultural to political nations obviously obscures the complex historical circumstances through which particular nation states emerged and have been able to present the link between state and nation.[31] Pearson (1994) has drawn attention to arguments concerning the distinction between nation states and state nations. The nation state is the political entity that emerges as a result of claims by an ethnic nation (invented or otherwise) for political autonomy, whereas the state nation promotes the image of a national community for purposes of state-legitimation. Thus one key difference between modern states is the degree to which they were formed as a result of nationalist movements from below, or through the imposition of particular public symbolic statements on the part of existing political authorities. In terms of the consciousness of citizens it seems likely that both possibilities operate within the boundaries of any particular national territory. Italy and Germany, created as unified polities in 1861 and 1871 respectively, certainly had to work to produce viable images of the nation. But in practice the older states such as Britain and France also had to deal with complex internal heterogeneity in the creation of external images of national culture.[32] In this sense it is interesting to note that those who feel that the contemporary nation state is in crisis because of the disintegration of political and cultural constituencies are perpetuating a somewhat naïve assumption that such integration ever existed.

My argument on the nation state echoes the discussion in Chapter 2 of the processes through which social anthropology as a discipline has found itself in crisis over the viability of central theoretical constructs which never were intended to be other than heuristic abstractions. Once again the problem appears to centre on the effect of rendering explicit the complex relationships through which the nation state is sustained as an image and as a social entity. In the case of the nation state, it is the easy incorporation of explicit counter-discourses into official discourse which interests me. There are an increasing number of studies that draw attention to alternative contemporary communities which do not reproduce the model of the named territorial unit, with a specific and coherent cultural identity, yet the findings of such studies are not necessarily debilitating or challenging the dominant position of the nation state in late twentieth century political and economic life.

Hannerz (1993), for example, has suggested that previous notions of the national are being displaced by other kinds of imagined transnational communities, made up of occupational or religious groups or adherents to particular youth styles of dress or music. The subjective experiences of spatial uprootedness, of migration and hybridity are now being voiced as a challenge to previous paradigms which normalized stable, coherent, territorialized identities. Malkki writes about Hutu refugees in Tanzania, stateless, displaced subjects who are involved in constructing national traditions for themselves as a challenge to the states that see them as 'categorical anomalies thus dangerous in both a politic and a symbolic sense' (Malkki 1990: 33). Verdery's work on Romania also stresses the tension between concepts of the nation and the state under socialist rule (Verdery 1991a and 1991b). She notes that for western nation states the processes of state-building and nation-building are generally assumed to be complementary, while in Romania the nation was invoked against the processes of state-building (Verdery 1990). These ideas have also been thoroughly explored from within the domain of cultural studies.[33] Globalization itself is taken as a process which is typified by the ways in which cultural practices move out of specific spaces and languages – out of what were previously deemed their proper territories. Thus Young argues after Deleuze and Guattari:

> Where capitalism differs from earlier historical forms such as despotism is that it does not simply encode and therefore control desire: it has to operate through a double movement because it must first of all do away with the institutions and cultures that have already been developed. The basic need of capitalism is to engineer an encounter between the deterritorialized wealth of capital and the labour capacity of the deterritorialized worker.
>
> (Young 1995: 169)

Writers such as Gilroy and Hall have criticized the notion of national cultures in their work on diaspora, syncretism, creolization and the production of difference within previously demarcated imperial spaces. Appadurai in his discussion of ethnoscapes, financescapes, mediascapes, idioscapes, etc. has focused attention on movements and linkages in which contemporary subjectivities are constituted (Appadurai 1986). Other writers have taken a more radical stance and typified the globalizing processes of the late twentieth century as directed quite explicitly to the production of difference as a discrete form of agency with no necessary substantive content. Deleuze and Guattari insist that it is not the particular differences which Appadurai describes, nor the site of difference which interests writers such as Hall and Gilroy, nor even the erasure of difference as discussed by Baudrillard, but the productivity of difference that is crucial (Deleuze and Guattari 1972).

Teresa de Lauretis provides an analogy in her discussion of gender. Taking a constructivist position she argues that gender is a representation and that the representation of gender is its construction. However she goes a step further than many writers of this persuasion in her addition that:

the construction of gender is also effected by its deconstruction; that is to say, by any discourse, feminist or otherwise, that would discard it as ideological misrepresentation. For gender is not only the effect of representation but also its excess, what remains outside discourse as a potential trauma which can rupture or destabilize any representation.

(de Lauretis 1987: 3)

This bringing together, into a single analytical frame, of the constructivist approach and the awareness afforded by deconstruction, could thus be seen as a play between the implicit and explicit dimensions of any social form without necessarily implying a radical questioning of premises which are in fact foundational to both positions. This was Strathern's point in her identification of the underlying premise of culture as construct (see Chapter 2) and in the context of this chapter, is also Kapferer's point as he stresses the inherently ambivalent relationship between state and nation in egalitarian nationalism and the tradition of philosophical liberalism on which it depends. Thus, while the state achieves its integrity in the will of the nation and of the people, the integrity of persons as autonomous and discrete individuals is always potentially threatened by the will of this greater collectivity (Kapferer 1988: 7).

It is thus not surprising that the ambivalence of the relationship between state and nation was itself on view at the Expo'92, as there is no ultimate paradox in the nation state producing images of itself that appear to undermine the foundations of the institution, just as social anthropology as a discipline can use the possibilities afforded by reflexivity to reinforce rather than undermine disciplinary specificity. The possibility of such effects is nevertheless both fascinating and culturally specific and, to my mind, is itself an apt subject of anthropological enquiry. To look, ethnographically, at how the nation state operates at universal exhibitions, is thus to look once again at the relationship which philosophical liberalism has produced for the lived experience of twentieth-century Europeans; that is the relationship between very particular representational strategies through which we attempt to define who we are, and practically constituted ideas which may or may not support our representational fantasies, but which are nevertheless bound to engage with them in some way.[34]

Chapter 4

The universal exhibition: changing relationships between technology and culture

Everything, then, depends upon this: that we ponder the question concerning technology and continue to watch over it. How can this happen? Above all through our catching sight of what comes to presence in technology, instead of merely staring at the technological. So long as we represent technology as an instrument, we remain held fast.

(Heidegger 1977: 32)

THE NATION AND THE CORPORATION

Itself a product of machine technology, the Great International Exhibition of 1851 celebrated capital and empire. In this first 'global' exhibit, mass production was on show in the very fabric of the event. Subsequent exhibitions developed on the basis of these beginnings and by the late nineteenth century the institution had reached its apogee. The idea of totalizing paradigms, and the full and 'physical realization of previous knowledge' in the exhibits was firmly established as the ideal form (Greenhalgh 1989: 89). Culture and technology were the objects of display, economic and political power the motivations for the very costly sponsorship of participation. Until the First World War such exhibitions were defined not only by their scope, but also by their optimism, their extravagance and their spirit of international competition.

As the exhibitions grew so too the categories of participation changed. The earliest universal exhibitions were not overtly concerned with the display of the nation state but with defining the material conditions of a civilized and progressive life-style through the accumulation and classification of those elements required for its construction. In 1851 the principal categories of display were: raw materials, heavy machinery, food products, liberal arts, agriculture and horticulture, fine arts, decorative products, chemical products, oil and electricity, transportation and communication, education, health and social life (Benedict 1983: 28). The competition between nations was couched in terms of the goods that each produced in these categories and the organizing nation could thus determine the criteria through which others would compete.

The move to a display of the nation itself was a gradual process, as national cultures, histories and future prospects came to be objectified and displayed in the ways described in Chapter 3. National business corporations operated as signifiers in this process. Ford and Singer were themselves cultural products of the United States, part of the national heritage and evidence of progressive modernization. Furthermore, private corporations were always active sponsors of these events, investing large sums of money in producing a stage for the display of their products. The interests of the nation and the corporation went hand in hand:

> London's Great Exhibition of 1851 demonstrated the achievements of the Industrial Revolution and the importance of Britain therein. The French exhibitions in the nineteenth century asserted the cultural, political and economic cast of the country. The 1958 Exhibition confirmed Europe's recovery from the Second World War and launched the challenge of European unity from its future capital, Brussels. The most recent, held in Osaka in 1970, announced Japan's emergence as a world technological power.
>
> (Expo'92 Official Guide: 16)

Here we have strong statements about the relative importance and contributions of particular nation states to a developing world economy. Spain stressed that the 1992 exhibition should also be interpreted in this way:

> The Universal Exhibition means for our country the opportunity to appear before the international community as a modern, efficient country, capable of organizing a project of the size of the Exhibition. A country with competitive businesses and a highly-qualified labour force, capable of involving all economic sectors and public administrations in a common project.
>
> (Expo'92 Press Dossier)

The status of particular nation states is thus linked to business
expertise (with implicit technological back-up). In addition
the ability to display products that are both novel (and thus
unique) and useful beyond the local national market is so integral to the internal competition between national participants
that a history of the institution can be written in the following
terms:

> The great exhibitions hailed the innovations and advances of
> Mankind. London's 1851 exhibition displayed industrial
> machinery, the Colt revolver and the lawn mower. The public
> was informed about oil and aluminium in Paris in 1867. Visitors
> to Philadelphia in 1876 were presented with Bell's telephone,
> Edison's telegraph, the first sewing machines and type-
> writers. . . . Electric light shone in Barcelona in 1888 and Paris
> in 1889. Mass-produced Ford cars were the highlight in San
> Francisco in 1915. Television (Chicago 1933), nylon and plastics
> (New York 1939), the structure of the atom (Brussels 1958),
> the laser beam (Montreal 1967).
>
> (Expo'92 Official Guide: 17)

The close connection between business and culture ensured the
salience of national contributions to the history of mankind.

As the general exhibit halls gave way to the national pavilions,
so the manufacturers and particularly the multinational corporations began to construct their own exhibition spaces and by
the 1930s exhibition sites were dominated by national and corporate pavilions (Benedict 1983: 19). It was technological developments themselves which changed the nature of the international
exhibitions in subsequent decades, reducing their importance in
the public eye and altering their internal appearance. The wonder
of seeing things for the first time was diminished by the spread of
communications technologies which gave immediate mass access
to innovation via other channels such as newspapers, radios and
more recently television. The economic benefits for exhibitors
had increasingly to be measured against the advantages of more
widespread and effective advertising media and the more specialized trade fair. Finally, it has been claimed that increasingly since
the 1950s, world fairs seemed to have lost that central element
of international competition and have become simply business
fairs and amusement parks (Benedict 1983: 59):

[T]he growth of multinational corporations vitiated the character of world's fairs ... the multinationals grew at the expense of general exhibit halls, state and even national pavilions. Thus world's fairs were turning into trade fairs.

(Benedict 1983: 60)

However, the corporate presence at the Expo'92 complicates this view somewhat. If we look at the corporate presence at the Expo'92 there were four principal modes of participation. In the first place there was the massive corporate sponsorship of the national participants. The visibility of such sponsors varied from pavilion to pavilion. In the case of the United Kingdom, British Steel had a high profile as principal sponsor, to the extent that staff working there referred to the pavilion as the British Steel pavilion. A sailing yacht carrying the name and logo of the company stood alongside the pavilion and was seen by all visitors at the end of their pavilion tour. In many other cases corporate sponsors were simply acknowledged on the written leaflets available but not always seen by visitors. A variation on this kind of sponsorship was that taken by several multinationals who sponsored more than one national pavilion, giving funds to nations where their subsidiaries or branches were operating. And there were companies that operated both the above strategies. Coca-Cola, for example, had contributed to the US and the British pavilions as discussed in Chapter 3, and Coca-Cola (Spain) was one of the official sponsors of the Expo'92. However it was only the US pavilion which used the Coca-Cola logo as a discreet but visible part of its display of national culture.

Finally there were companies which participated as 'independent' (i.e. non-national) entities. At Expo'92 these high-profile corporate groups were the giants of the communications industries such as Siemens, Rank Xerox, Fujitsu, Sony and Alcatel. These companies acted both as official sponsors of the Expo and as participants in their own right. In this latter capacity they presented themselves as equivalent entities to the national participants. They produced images of corporate culture and history and emphasized their multiculturalism and their uniqueness within a certain competitive set of values. They had a day dedicated to them, equivalent to the national days celebrated by the other participants. They could not anchor their identity to specific territories, they had no flags or anthems, but the corporate pavilions and the general nature of their displays were so similar to those of the participating nation states that as entities, they appeared of a kind. The visitor experienced no change either of scale or of kind in moving between national and corporate pavilions. Of the six corporate participants who mounted their own pavilions in the international zone of the exhibition site, there were three high-profile multinational companies, Fujitsu, Siemens and Rank Xerox.[1] Despite their independent status as participants, these companies were not entirely divorced from their national setting. In each case they were in fact sited in such a way as to complement the exhibit mounted by their country of origin. Thus the Fujitsu high-tech spherical cinema stood opposite Japan's wooden pavilion. Siemens stood next door to Germany, Rank Xerox opposite the United States.

There was thus a relationship of interdependence between the corporate and national participants. The nation states and the multinationals operated as contexts for each other, each dependent on the presence of the other for the generation of particular effects. Universal expositions have always been explicitly concerned to display the nation state in a global context and to produce a particular relationship between political economy and culture. The presence of, and implicit association with, multinational companies allowed certain nation states to evoke a scope of global connection and an ethos of global concern that is hard to display convincingly within the confines of a strictly national display. The multinationals in turn could more effectively manifest their freedom from the constraints of national frontiers in a context where such frontiers were also on display.

The corporate participants have thus not in fact erased the centrality of national participation at universal exhibitions. However, the nature of their participation has had its effect. One of the most significant changes is the move away from the central display of the products of manufacturing industry to an ubiquitous but not always visible presence of communications industries. The possibilities afforded by contemporary communications technology has in turn altered the nature of international competition at the world fairs. Thus while Chapter 3 discussed some of the ways in which nations have harnessed universalist histories to national ones, so too we find the harnessing of national identities to corporate ends.

THE DISPLAY OF SURPLUS VALUE

Benedict (1983) noted that since the original Crystal Palace Exhibition of 1851, world fairs have been about selling goods and ideas. Participants sought to make money by stimulating markets and boosting trade, but they also looked to produce associations between consumer items and the cultural aspirations of an emergent bourgeoisie. Particular cultural values were thus displayed as evidence of human progress. The acquisition of culture in these material terms was presented in a moral context as the European nations displayed the goods as marks of civilization against the comparative backdrop of the dominated territories of Empire. These distant lands produced raw materials from which the western nations produced the evidence of their superior civilization.

This claim to a superior civilization thus rested on an ability to generate and display wealth. As Marx asserted, the wealth of capitalist production presents itself in the accumulation of commodities. The *display* of these products in venues such as world fairs emphasized exchange rather than use value, which in turn reinforced the link between civilized culture and those economies that generated surplus value (Benjamin 1978: 152).[2]

Gigantism, miniaturization and the self-conscious play with the symbolic have been the most common techniques through which objects have been, since 1851, transformed into icons of excess for display at universal exhibitions. Examples of all these techniques are quite well known. The exhibition monuments such as the Eiffel Tower and the Statue of Liberty, are among the most enduring examples of gigantism, but this technique has also consistently been used in temporary displays of national produce. Take for example the Oregon apple from the Panama Pacific International Exposition: '12 feet high with a panorama of the Hood River Valley within it' or the 'real cheese from New York state weighing eleven thousand pounds' (Benedict 1983: 17). It is not just the monuments or local exaggerations that are of note in this respect but also the obsessive measuring through which equivalence is established and the comparative importance of such exhibits assessed.

The centrality of competition encouraged the memorable excesses of the great world fairs of the late nineteenth and early twentieth century. Hillel Schwartz (1993) gives the example of a young American, Steele Mackaye, who conceived but never

Figure 8 On the roof of the Mexican pavilion
Source: Penelope Harvey

actually built, a vast kinematic spectatorium for the Columbian Exposition in Chicago in 1893. The idea was to mount twenty-five telescopic stages on six miles of railroad track, on which a six-act historical drama, entitled *The Great Discovery* or *The World Finder*, was to be performed essentially without spoken words in full view of 9,000 people. These practices continue today. Monuments are still constructed, large sums of money invested and the scale of the event measured in all conceivable terms, from the number of people passing through the turnstiles to the miles of cabling used in the installation of information systems. However the gigantism that makes the greatest impact in today's world fairs is of a different order from that of the last century and is associated particularly with film technology. Thus at the Expo'92 we found the Sony Jumbotron video screen standing eight storeys high on the Sony Plaza; the Alcatel Space Cinema, with its huge hemispheric auditorium projecting film ten times larger than normal cinema format, and the presentations of Fujitsu, Canada, Venezuela, Australia and Spain which will be discussed in more detail below.

The enjoyment of display and the ways in which objects are rendered available to a viewer's gaze was also evident in the equally prolific use of miniaturization. Mexico provided one such exhibit. On the roof of the pavilion, scaled models of ancient Meso-American buildings, miniature temples and houses, enabled the visitor to walk into the past (Figure 8). But it was France that for me produced the most impressive exhibition of this kind.

The entrance to the French pavilion was on the top floor of a large three-storey building. This upper room was lined with cabinets filled with examples of French cultural production, evidence of France's high culture, particularly all that is associated with literature, opera, history and the scientific discoveries of the Enlightenment (from ancient geometry to holograms). The floor of this room was of glass. The drop, which was visible, was broken by a model of eighteenth century Paris. Visitors stood on the glass floor and looked down through 200 years of French history. As they walked, they walked over a model of the city, in fact over layers of cities from different periods. Many people, including myself, were a bit nervous about walking on the floor – the drop induced vertigo. At the far end of the room there were televisions, holograms and computers with more information

Figure 9 Inside the French pavilion
Source: Paris Match Spécial Seville 1992: 74 (photograph by Litron)

available from the video-disks on the Paris exhibition of 1900, a contemporary form of miniaturization and accessibility.

Down on the second floor the model of the French city reappeared at shoulder height (Figure 9). As we walked backwards in time through the exhibit, it was clear that the model was in fact hanging upside down and reflected in a mirror. What had been seen from above, and what could still be seen by looking to the side and down was the mirror image, inverted. This was the pavilion of mirror technology. The ground floor was dominated by the mirrored film pit. The films were used to advertise French companies and the research they had sponsored as their contribution to 'our world of the future'. I watched a film about space which depicted the world as watched by a satellite, setting off from Spain looking over America: communications technology uniting the globe. As the film played, as well as watching it from around the pit, people were floating over it on a moving walkway. Some walked backwards to prolong the experience, or came in from the wrong end to walk through it slowly, against the force of the walkway.

I began to feel that the vertigo you felt on stepping onto the glass floor at the top of the pavilion was a planned prefiguration of the vertigo you would feel as a result of the intellectual free fall which was about to take place as you entered this hyper-reflexive exhibit.

As this display well illustrates, both gigantism and miniaturization are produced in a context where designers are heavily involved in the self-conscious play with the symbolic. The Expo'92 produced countless examples of displays which contained complex layers of references both in the architecture and the contents of pavilions, to previous times and places, and even to previous exhibitions. Reflexivity was intrinsic to the Expo design. In these various ways exhibitions today, as previously, offer memorable instances of excess, of dramatic changes in scale and of playful allusion to the mobility of cultural signifiers. The relentless urge for the minds of consumers has always motivated exhibitors; what has changed over the past century are the ways in which gigantism, miniaturization and symbolic allusion are used to reach these consumers.

Impressed by this aspect of late twentieth century exhibitions, Umberto Eco characterized the distinction between today's fairs and those of the last century in somewhat different terms to those of Benedict. His observation was that while nineteenth century exhibitions displayed goods, contemporary exhibitions simply display themselves. Distinguishing symbolic and utilitarian function, he claimed with reference to the Montreal Fair of 1967 that: 'The basic ideology of an exposition is that the packaging is more important than the product, meaning that the building and the objects in it should communicate the value of a culture, the image of a civilization' (Eco 1983: 299).

However, as I have argued in Chapter 3, the Expo'92 shows us that we are not dealing with an institution that has changed to the extent that either Benedict or Eco assume. We are dealing with a hybrid institution that for better or worse carries clear traces of its origins. There are important continuities with the ethos and even the form of previous exhibitions, and these sit unproblematically alongside what might appear to be paradoxical and opposing alternatives. Thus, just as the nation state is both constructed and deconstructed in the contemporary exhibition, so too we find that the relationship between the utilitarian and the symbolic is intrinsic to contemporary displays. Before moving to a more detailed discussion of this topic I will first return to Eco's observation on packaging and the communication of value and image.

In Chapter 3 I argued that the universal exhibition renders its participating entities equivalent by acting as a venue for the generation and display of commensurable difference. In so far as the fairs are promoting and selling the idea of this kind of cultural difference, they necessarily have to face the permanent marketing challenge of producing such difference in easily consumable form. In this sense universal expositions are fundamentally comparative events, both with their former manifestations and within their own particular confines, and the comparison is overtly competitive. Competition generates distinction yet it brings its own problems, for competitors have always faced each other 'using very similar techniques of display . . . competition bred a kind of uniformity in display . . . the more alike competitors became, the more fiercely they competed. Conversely, the more fiercely they competed, the more alike they became (Benedict 1983: 15).

A fear of international uniformity was being voiced incidentally as early as the 1867 Paris Fair. At the Expo'92 the individual pavilions were in competition for visitors and popularity ratings and there was much comparison not just by visitors but also by the participants themselves. Thus we discover that Australia's Barrier Reef is 'the world's largest living thing', and Chile's 'Millenarian Iceberg' evidence that the Chileans could export anything anywhere, even a huge chunk of Antarctica to the sweltering heat of a Sevillian summer. Ireland proudly announced that it had won the competition for the best logo and there were constant tallies of the numbers of visitors passing through the different venues. A consumer-led informal ranking of the pavilions established Canada, Fujitsu, Venezuela and Spain as the world's new superpowers. The problem for the participants is that the tactics of simultaneous co-operation and competition, while they sustain the possibility of difference, tend also to mitigate against the expression of any distinctive cultural content.

This situation is exacerbated by the influence of multinational corporations in contemporary exhibitions. As I have indicated above, the major multinationals participating as exhibitors in Seville were involved in the production and use of communications technology. The specificity of this kind of corporate presence raises a question about the significance of the move away from the displays of the products of the manufacturing industries which sustained the image of a world made up of discrete nation states, and which stood as a concrete indication of a nation's technological capacity. Greenhalgh has pointed out that the pre-First World War imperial exhibitions were about 'the celebration of high capital, as enhanced by machine technology' (Greenhalgh 1989: 94). The post-imperial exhibition still celebrates capital, but enhancement is now through electronic communications technology. What difference does this make? Has the nation state been reduced to packaging, merely the symbolic effect produced for the benefit of multinational corporations?

We have looked in Chapter 3 at how national governments invest in image and seek to display particular aspects of the relationship between nation states and West European capitalism. We need also to consider some of the ways in which multinational corporations used the image of national identity as part of the cut-throat business of generating difference in a world of increasing market integration. The idea relates to what Hannerz (1993) has written about the workings of international companies in the late twentieth century. He has pointed out how global corporations need to loosen their ties to particular countries. Multinationals, he argues, need to construct their own systems of value, an international language, and even a history and mythology of the past. Businesses can now think of themselves as having cultures, ways of doing things that are no longer grounded in territory, landscapes, peoples or even tradition as commonly understood.

Such a position resonates with the way in which a company such as Fujitsu presents itself as operating in a 'world where the only frontiers are in your mind'; in which Siemens talks of its 'tradition of innovation', and Coca-Cola objectifies its association with the United States while actively sponsoring other nations which have come to constitute local markets for its product.

Chapter 3 showed various ways in which the generic notion of the nation is both reinforced and transgressed in the national exhibits. Here my interest is in how the objectification of national culture in a comparative and competitive environment undermines the notion of essence in ways that evoke and complement the marketing strategies of multinational companies. At Expo'92 it was possible to see the idea of a national culture as essence existing alongside an altogether different view of culture as an outcome, a technological effect that was no longer nation specific.

CULTURE AS TECHNOLOGICAL EFFECT

One very common way in which this occurred was through the use of film technology. One of the main principles that has historically rendered nation states equivalent has been the link between nation and territory (Hobsbawm 1990). In apparent deference to this value, several of the participants presented films of national landscapes as the centre-piece of their exhibits. Indeed where innovative film technologies were used, such presentations were among the highlights of the Expo displays. Chapter 3 made reference to the Spanish Moviemax, the film distinguished by chairs which moved in synchrony with the action. Venezuela produced dramatic effects with a large screen and landscape shots which combined majestic beauty and thrilling fast-paced sequences in which viewers felt as if they were shooting the rapids and parachuting over the massive waterfall of Salto del Angel. Canada used IMAX high-resolution technology and a giant screen to deliver images 'so vivid you can even see normal skin moisture on faces'. Australia screened a 360-degree film 'placing the audience in the middle of never-ending expanses of sandy beach, painted dancing Aborigines, a jostling herd of sheep, careering kangaroos and charging cattle'.

Despite the occasional culturally or geographically specific reference, what distinguished these films from each other and from the offerings of other nations was their technology, not the landscapes. Beaches, waterfalls, mountain ranges are standard venues for today's landscape photographers. For the Expo public, the aesthetics of a beautiful view, or the excitement of white water and steep vertigo-inducing drops, were the same whether viewed in Australia, Canada, Venezuela or Spain. Furthermore, all these participants were concerned to show the geographical and cultural diversity of their national territories. Venezuela presented images of the nation under the slogan 'difference unites us'. This theme of the unifying potential of difference was applied equally to the relationships of their various peoples as to the contrasting ecologies of their land. The familiar banner of multiculturalism, the theme of unity in diversity which so many nations appealed to, could thus be used interchangeably in reference to peoples: 'indians, whites and blacks joined in a single being', and to landscapes: 'sun and shade, sea and desert', all part of the same national territory. Similarly national character was linked to climate. Caracas was presented as a multicultural city, yet its people have one thing in common, the fact that their characters reflect the warmth of the climate in which they live. Such clichés were commonplace and, not surprisingly, their effect on the audiences had more to do with the form of their delivery than with the content of what was said. Venezuela was a very popular show because of the film technology, not because of its message of cultural unity or because anybody thought that by watching the film they had learnt a great deal about Venezuela as a nation.

These glossy travel films illustrate how landscapes were presented as instances of natural cultural heritage alongside the histories, products, and national symbols discussed in more detail in Chapter 3. The notion of a landscape as both constitutive and expressive of national character was one which was formed in the eighteenth century and became established as an idea in the nineteenth century. Furthermore this process was occurring at a time when an incipient tourist industry was introducing the possibility of packaging and promoting views, scenic routes and typical landscapes (Sears 1989).[3] National parks, an American-led innovation of the nineteenth century, objectified particular scenic possibilities (Lofgren 1993: 62). The value of these territories to the nation lay in the fact that they were supposedly imbued with an essential, foundational spirit. The nation had a duty to preserve these landscapes from the forces of modernization which might, through the speed of change, remove the visible traces of the nation's most foundational heritage, the land. The possibilities for the recognition of such landscapes were of course the outcomes of a range of representational processes. Images in museums and galleries, geography lessons in school, tourist promotions, and even events such as a pilgrimage, could lead people to associate particular landscapes with specific national characteristics, until images of the landscape become blended with their experience. At such a point it requires only an iconic image to evoke a particular sovereign territory (Lofgren 1993: 178–9):

> In a world where fewer and fewer identities are based on the clear-cut pedagogy of space, the nation state provides an absolute space.... The national territory is also territorialized in a very powerful way, while the landscape is projected (rather anachronistically) into history.
>
> (Lofgren 1993: 191–2)

However, the problem is that once packaged as sensational images, the specificity of such spaces disappears and we are left with the juxtaposition of landscapes as formative of national genius (the rationale for the use of such images as the centre-pieces of national exhibits), and landscapes designed to elicit sensation, sensations enhanced by the film technologies I have referred to above. Once again the competition between nations at the Expo is played out in terms of a search for sensation and technological effect that in practice diminishes the differences between nations in terms of the substantive content of their displays.

Once it is established that nation states are involved in the processes of marketing themselves through the production of particular (and arbitrary) images, it becomes easier to understand a further dynamic in the relationship between nation states and multinational companies. I refer here to the process of product differentiation and brand recognition. If, in the mid-nineteenth century and early twentieth century the nation was quite obviously the product of international politics, it is now possible at the end of the twentieth century to see that the nation is also the product of international capital. Difference is produced and marketed in the same ways as other consumer goods, and nations can even acquire a kind of brand identity which can be brought into the service of selling other products. In a fascinating discussion of the Benetton advertising campaign, Lury has argued that brand identity is about owning an essence. This essence is what distinguishes one product from another, the real thing from the copy. Coca-Cola is one of many cola drinks, but its advertising campaigns seek to establish that there is only one real brand of cola; the imitations are not essentially the same. However, brand identity is threatened by its own success: if a brand becomes generic, as was the case with the biro, then it loses that specificity which ensures its privileged position in the market. Indeed Coca-Cola's decision to reassert its brand identity with the slogan 'It's the Real Thing', was presumably taken in a market in which cola was in danger of becoming a generic product (Lury n.d. (1)).

If we return to the relationship between multinationals and nation states it is interesting to follow Lury's argument as to how particular products establish their brand identity with reference to national characteristics.[4] Swatch watches, for example, use the Swiss logo, and thereby evoke an implicit connection to a tradition of precision engineering and craftsmanship, itself associated with national characteristics. However, the interesting thing about branding is that once you have a brand, the market can be redefined. Swatch watches are not in fact sold as enduring, reliable timepieces (this characteriztic is implicit in their Swissness). A Swatch is not just a watch but an accessory, comparable to a piece of jewellery. It is a fashion item, and a buyer might want to own several to wear with different outfits or to reflect different moods or personal characteristics. The essence, the enduring precision of Swiss watch engineering, is made to sit alongside images which in fact transgress the genre; a watch as fashion item, disposable, replaceable, ephemeral.

Thus successful branding is not simply about the ownership of essence but is at the same time about the estrangement of genre. A successful brand is not typical of its kind; it is both of a kind and transgressive of that kind. What Lury shows so well in her fascinating discussion of Benetton is the way in which this company, to a far greater degree than Swatch, has produced a brand that is essentially about generic estrangement. Here there is no reference to national characteristics but to an imaginary global community. The Benetton advertisements set out to shock, to produce images of differences that are improbably reconciled. The possibility of reconciliation is presented as a simple consumer choice. The company catchphrase, 'the united colors of Benetton', is used alongside images that seek to transgress 'natural' categories, particularly those of sexuality and race. The Benetton brand achieves visibility in the market through the estrangement of genre in the face of its blatant assertion. This branding technique no longer refers to the product (as was the case with Swatch); Benetton seeks simply to become a selling space in a market for consumer goods.[5] That space can be filled by any product that Benetton wants to sell, and will sell as long as they are successful in marketing their brand image.

It is in this regard that we might reconsider the relationships between international business interests and nation states at contemporary universal exhibitions. Nation states are required to market themselves, make themselves visible in a saturated market, project an essence and transgress a genre. We have seen in the previous chapters how particular nations transgress the genre of the territorial, sovereign, monoculture and how these transgressions take place in the face of their blatant assertion. The Swiss proclamation 'je pense donc je suisse', becomes a more complex statement in this regard, simultaneously denying the possibility of a national essence and stating that such a denial *is itself* a possibility afforded by the fact of being Swiss. Switzerland could, in this regard, be seen as adopting a position similar to the executives of the Benetton company, seeking to establish a brand identity based on generic estrangement.

Given the fact that universal exhibitions are primarily concerned with the promotion of national products and the facilitation of business relationships (including most crucially those linked to the tourist industry), we might now see the presentation of the nation state at these fairs as attempts by representatives of particular business interests to create and project brand identities for the nation, identities which can then be used to sell any product that might find a way to take advantage of such an image. Governments collude with such business interests as they are, after all, those most closely involved with the co-ordination of the 'economy' that such activities generate.[6]

TECHNOLOGY AND CULTURE

Throughout the history of world fairs the political and economic motivations and agendas have been underplayed in the displays of technology, art and science which are presented as the universal goals and values of human endeavour. In this sense, as I have argued, the world fairs have a deep and intrinsic commitment to the values of modernism. However, technological developments have produced a situation in which these values are easily undermined, particularly in the possibilities they afford for certain kinds of postmodernist expression, such as that characterized by Featherstone as 'the celebration of the depthlessness of culture, the decline of the originality/genius of the artistic producer and the assumption that art can only be repetition' (Featherstone 1991: 8). I have tried to show the ways in which the modern and the postmodern existed at the Expo'92. My interest here is to look at how contrasting relationships between technology and culture create these contrary effects.

Invisible techniques of assistance for the expression of cultural forms

The most conservative manifestation of this relationship is the display of 'high culture', valuable original pieces, in high-tech exhibition spaces. The technologies behind the display of high culture are invisible techniques of assistance designed to enable the fullest expression of the beauty of the cultural form. The Expo site contained several exhibits which brought culture and technology together in this way: the Pavilion of the Fifteenth Century, the Treasures of Spain (within the Spanish pavilion), and the art collection at the Holy See in the Vatican pavilion. Authentic indigenous art was most prominently represented by the Gold Exhibition in the American Plaza and the Treasures of Nigeria in the African Plaza.

The Pavilion of Art and Culture around 1492 contained an exquisite display of late fifteenth century pieces. The gallery space was itself an art object, the restored fifteenth century Carthusian monastery where Columbus is known to have stayed and where his remains were once held. This building is described as the 'nerve centre' of the universal exposition, the 'symbolic focal point', which served as a tangible, concrete historical presence in an event which was otherwise comprised of only semi-permanent structures, most of which would be dismantled. History in this exhibit was presented through a display of original forms in contrast to the use elsewhere of models and mirrors and a pervasive state of the art technology such as high-resolution television, IMAX and spherical projection, holograms and virtual reality. The technology is of course there in the 1492 exhibit, in the control of light, heat and humidity, in the restoration of the building and in the transport and surveillance of the objects. However, it was the art objects not the technology which visitors were invited to wonder at. In this conservative model technology is used to reveal latent truth or beauty but is not in any way modifying the intrinsic cultural form.

Innovations and improving cultural life

An alternative relationship between technology and culture is that of liberal rationalist thought which posits culture as a way of life and technology as innovation and improvement. In this model there is a causal and developmental relationship between technology and culture. Several pavilions explored this relationship.

The Italians, for example, had mounted an exhibit on perspective, which discussed and illustrated the new theories and laws of vision which altered notions of reality in the fifteenth century. They then suggested that that sense of reality was itself challenged by contemporary technology. In what appeared to be a booth to listen to the high quality sound of an operatic performance which you could also watch on screen, visitors unknowingly allowed themselves to be filmed, and their image as viewers was played back on banked television screens just out of their sight. It was not clear who was watching and who was being watched, nor indeed what exactly anyone was looking at. Following the exhibit on perspective the visitor entered a display which discussed the relationship between communication technologies, memory and culture. Devices such as the eye-glass and the pendulum were presented as objects designed to thwart space and time. Paper was shown to have acted as the main support for human memory and culture until the recent move into the electronic age where hypertexts hold millions of pieces of information in computerized systems. The message was that technologies designed for medical and military purposes affect the generation of cultural knowledges more widely.

The Siemens exhibit was even more explicit about this connection between communications technology and contemporary cultural practices. Siemens, one of the high-profile corporate participants, was the supplier of the communications system to the Expo site and had also led the German–Spanish consortium responsible for the electrical engineering and the installation of telecommunications equipment for the high-speed rail link from Madrid to Seville.

The Siemens exhibit was focused on company history, on corporate culture, 'the evolution of technology at Siemens from the pioneering days to modern innovations'. This was a company with a tradition of innovation and its multi-media exhibit was a survey of the history of electrical engineering, electronics and microelectronics as they have affected the world of work. The tradition which the exhibit evoked was one of innovation. Evolutionary change was presented as progress, rather than adaptation, a natural process of development through which the quality of life is enhanced. A history is presented in which transformations in communications technologies developed until isolated systems reached their limits. Then came the most recent transformation, the evolution of networks and the merging of systems. The message of this exhibit was that if we use our technical resources properly a utopian future lies within our reach. We cannot predict the future, it mused, but we can invent it.

The other distinctive message that the Siemens pavilion stressed was the need to recognize and reinforce the symbiosis of man, nature and technology. The greater the connection, the less environmental damage or waste of energy. In fact its film stated quite explicitly that the human race will destroy itself if it does not learn to act in the terms of integrated systems. Technical progress was explicitly rendered analogous to biological process as the theme of 'Evolutionary networks, technology and biology in parallel' was expounded. This message was picked up in the ecological responsibility embraced by the company, its involvement in searches for alternative sources of energy and its commitment to use the potential of technological evolution in the service of mankind. Its call was for holistic thinking to avoid the conflicts that have arisen between man, nature and technology in the past.

Siemens, it boasted, is the company which has made it possible to do away with monotonous and arduous work, enhancing the flexibility and efficiency of the productive process. It is involved in developing networked transport systems and modern electromedical technologies.

The general themes of the Siemens exhibit were echoed in that of Rank Xerox:

> The role of the individual, his human values and his functioning within his social, cultural and economic context is a vital one in creating a better future for coming generations. Communication is a key factor in all this. And what is the essential tool for storing and transmitting knowledge, experience, even the ephemeral qualities of poetry? Unquestionably, the written word, the document.
>
> (Expo'92 Official Guide: 245)

Rank Xerox, the official supplier of the office computer systems to the Expo, presented a multimedia rendition of the history of documentation. Again the process was evolutionary. This time visitors watched a video of the evolution of the written word that pointed towards the possibility of a fantastic future. They had a copy of the message which was launched by satellite into space in the hope that an extraterrestrial might one day find it, interpret it and visit Earth.

In these examples it is clear that there is an integral relationship between technology and culture. Human history is the history of technological development. Neither Rank Xerox nor Siemens made reference to the nation state in their historical approach to the development of technological systems. These systems developed as if in isolation from their specific economic and political environments, just as the specificity of the emergence of particular nation states was not referred to in the national exhibits. Without a specific social context through which to evaluate the social effects of such progress, the technology is presented as a neutral agent in the pursuit of improved life-styles for the human race in general.

All the multinational exhibits stressed the ways in which the technologies which they were responsible for producing and which they were promoting at the Expo, were technologies which operated for the benefit of humanity generally, for the global community in which the deterritorialized multinationals operate.

The attitude of the Fujitsu personnel was particularly strong in this regard. Despite my insistence, the personnel officer denied the importance of the special relationship between Japan and Fujitsu. They were not serving the partial interests of particular constituencies, nor were they engaged in the nightmares of modernist technological development, developments in which technology stood in opposition to art, replacing and working against human and spiritual values. The presentation of technology at world fairs was ever thus, as Rydell has noted:

> The century-of-progress fairs represented a powerful defense of corporate capitalism as a modernizing agency that would lead America out of the depression towards a bountiful future. . . . Fundamental to this effort was an assault on remaining vestiges of values that were associated with what some historians have called a 'culture of production'. To hasten the dissolution of this older emphasis on restraint and inhibition, already under siege by world's fairs at the beginning of the century and by the steady barrage of advertising that saturated the country during the 1920s, world's fair builders injected their fantasies of progress with equally heavy doses of technological utopianism and erotic stimulation. In pavilions like 'Democracity' and 'Futurama' at the New York World's Fair, technology appeared as a democratizing force that would simultaneously require a cadre of experts to assure the rational operation of intersecting social, economic and political forces.
>
> (Rydell 1993: 117)

The idea of technology as a modernizing and democratizing force was, as you might now expect, contested in other Expo exhibits although there was no direct challenge to the transnational companies' presentation of themselves not merely as good global citizens but as guardians of life itself. The Dutch pavilion had mounted an exhibition of press photographs of world atrocities, the outcomes of certain uses of military technologies particularly in Europe and in the Gulf War. Needless to say the causes of war and the interests of the arms manufacturers were again not alluded to. But technological innovation was not presented as necessarily progressive or liberating. The display at the Pavilion of the Environment presented the problems that human activity has created in the environment, again using compelling

and innovative film technology, which presumably diverted attention from what these technologies presented.

Just as concepts of tradition and innovation are equally constitutive of the modern nation state, so too the conservative and
liberal models of the relationship between technology and culture
can co-exist without contradiction. Technological innovation is a
precondition for the preservation of antiquity, the distinction
between the ancient and the modern itself a hallmark of modernity. Progressive technologies enable history to be held stable,
to be preserved as a point of origin from which to measure
progress and change. The innovative and the traditional necessarily co-exist, each requiring the other for its own visibility.

Technology as cultural artefact

There was however a third way in which the relationship between
technology and culture appeared at the Expo. In this guise technology existed as cultural artefact in its own right. Here
technology is culture, not assisting or causing but substituting,
referring only back to itself. One of the Russian exhibits combined these last two possibilities and enabled their comparison.

The Novosibirsk Medical Research Centre presented
'HELIOS', a prognosis expert system in which man discovers
outer space in himself through the new cosmogony. The computer's heliogeophysical data bank, with an input of sixty to
seventy years of data, allowed you to reconstruct real outer-
space events at any time of your embryo development (for those
currently aged between fifteen and sixty-five). This information
enabled you to forecast the level of your biorhythms which are
dependent on these concrete heliogeophysical factors. Was this
an instance of knowledge and progress or an ironic collapse of
science and fantasy?

There were many more examples. The Canadians showed a
video montage, a blatant spoof on national promotional films.
'The taxpayer of Canada presents . . . another government movie',
ran the opening credit. National symbols were ridiculed, the
obligatory Mountie was a cardboard figure that collapsed on
screen. References to Canadian life were made in a style of
deliberate whimsy modernity. A woman cycled through a remote
rural landscape making calls on her cell phone. The modern igloo
was equipped with remote-control television, microwave and

telephone and the owner sat in the middle of the living-room floor, fishing through the ice. The spoof was on the way that nations tried to promote an image of themselves at Expo, and could even be seen as a take-off of the dramatic IMAX movie which followed in the central venue of the pavilion. Visitors were thus warned in advance that the images were simply artificial constructs.

By far the most spectacular exhibits at the Expo were those which offered sensation or experience with little or no specific cultural referent. People queued all day to watch the film in the Spanish pavilion where the seats moved to convey the sensations of movement associated with the images on the screen. The images were in the genre of the travel film, a variety of landscapes that could involve the visitor in hang-gliding, skiing, kayaking, and horse-riding. But the landscapes of Spain were not particular to Spain and were hard to distinguish from those of Australia, Venezuela and Canada, which also offered the big-screen experience. Finally there was the dramatic Fujitsu production, *Echoes of the Sun*, packed with technology that you could not see, yet here, unlike the 'Art and Culture' exhibit, it was the technology that people queued to experience. And it was the proximity of experience, not the distance offered by representation, that drew people to these displays:

> Discover the art in technology. And the technology in life. . . . Fujitsu welcomes you to a world where the only frontiers are in your mind, and where art, technology and life become one.
>
> (Expo'92 Official Guide: 240)

Fujitsu, the world's second largest manufacturer of information processing systems, generates telecommunications and microelectronic devices throughout the world. Its territory is global, its corporate population quantifiable: 145,000 employees worldwide, installing and manufacturing its systems in over 100 countries.

Working with the theme of art in technology, Fujitsu stunned Expo visitors with the computer-generated graphics of the process of photosynthesis and glycolysis, the basis of all life on Earth. The show, entitled *Echoes of the Sun* was the world's first IMAX SOLIDO TM, full-colour three-dimensional wrap-around motion picture, and it set out to show how the possibilities for human motion lie in sunlight. Visitors were immersed in images projected in three dimensions on a giant wrap-around screen. They watched the thirty-minute film wearing what were referred to as 'futuristic

3-D glasses'. The central figures of the film were three puppets, a chameleon, a caterpillar and a ladybird, living in a vineyard. Grapes dangled apparently within the reach of the viewer. As the story of how plants convert sunlight into energy progressed, viewers felt forced to duck to avoid the molecules, which hurtled towards them from the screen. Visitors screamed as the chameleon's tongue shot out towards each one of them as they watched.

Throughout the emphasis was on the possibilities that Fujitsu technology affords for making things visible. Thus, while the film renders visible a process not visible with the naked eye, so, they warn you, the film *Echoes of the Sun* is packed with technology that you cannot see. The guidebook to the pavilion in turn reveals this information. It contains explanations of how the images on the screen were produced. We see photographs of the puppeteers as well as details of how computers generate graphics. The complexity of the processes involved are stressed. These images are not photographs. We are in the presence of a technology that is not simply reproducing originals but generating idealized and imaginary forms, concrete versions of scientific abstractions which nevertheless can simulate the movements and the relationships of the original forms. The guidebook also explains how the three-dimensional glasses work, the effects of the wrap-around screen, even how a raccoon was rehearsed to walk over and eat a grape for one of the film sequences.

There were thus three relationships between technology and culture on show at the Expo'92: invisible techniques of assistance for the fullest expression of the beauty of authentic form; techniques of innovation and improvement for culture as a way of life; and technology as cultural artefact, providing sensational evidence of its own enterprise. These in turn entailed two basic representational paradigms. On the one hand there are technologies to represent the world, on the other technologies of simulation, provoking a reflexive awareness of artificiality and simulacra. The first of these conceives of technology as enabler, and is the concept that lies behind the notion of the Expo as a technology of nationhood. Technology enables a perspective that can produce wholeness from fragmentation. Expo enables the appearance of the world as a whole, through the revelation of the fragments that are cut from it and the apparent celebration of their differences. As Strathern has noted:

The realization that wholeness is rhetoric itself is relentlessly exemplified in collage, or collections that do not collect but display the intractability of the disparate elements. Yet such techniques of showing that things do not add up paradoxically often include not less cutting but more – a kind of hypercutting of perceived events, moments, impressions. And if elements are presented as so many cut-outs, they are inevitably presented as parts coming from other whole cloths, larger pieces, somewhere.

(Strathern 1991a: 110)

However this is not the end of the story because Expo is not simply a technology for producing wholeness through the emergence of apparently incommensurable fragments. It is also about spectacle, a process that does not produce its object by a cut from a ground that still remains as founding referent, but rather a process through which ground is in fact erased and all we are left with is culture, culture as the ubiquitous effect of social processes whose particular conditions of emergence are no longer visible.

The technique is quite familiar in contemporary art and is one which centres on the use of copies and discernible artifice to challenge essential identities and reveal constructs: Cindy Sherman's photographic series of self-portraits, for example, in which she dresses up in the guise of already-known feminine stereotypes:

Her self is understood as contingent upon the possibilities pro-vided by the culture in which Sherman participates, not by some inner impulse. As such, her photographs reverse the terms of art and autobiography. They use art not to reveal the artist's self, but to show the self as an imaginary construct. There is no real Cindy Sherman in these photographs; there are only the guises she assumes.

(Crimp 1993: 179)

Much of Expo's most spectacular technology of display works in this way: the laser show over the Lake of Spain in which computer-generated figures dance flamenco on the water; the Fujitsu three-dimensional cinemascope where the objects depicted hang before your eyes and where images move past you as you watch; the ubiquitous holograms, are all examples of these ethereal absent presences. The use of these technologies no longer aimed to represent the world as we know it to be. Instead, they celebrated the possibility of producing a simulated world, a world of images more real than the real, a fascination with the hyper-real, pretensions to realities that were never there in the first place or at least not in such perfect form, concrete manifestations of abstract possibilities.

We have returned here to the contrast between representation and interaction discussed in Chapter 2. It will be noted in this regard that representational technologies are those which provide context to render culture visible, while simulation technologies do not require context, they simply produce effect and in so doing they erase the social conditions of their production. Technology for Fujitsu is art; technologies generate beauty, they bring people together, enable communication, produce the essence of life itself as outcome not origin.

As Haraway has pointed out, 'micro-electronics is the technical basis of simulacra' (Haraway 1991: 165). These are technologies that take us into a world which Expo does not need to spell out; it simply exists through them. Haraway alludes to the pervasiveness of such effects:

Communications technologies depend on electronics. Modern states, multinational corporations, military power, welfare state apparatuses, satellite systems, political processes, fabrication of our imaginations, labour-control systems, medical constructions of our bodies, commercial pornography, the international division of labour, and religious evangelism depend intimately upon electronics.

(Haraway 1991: 165)

Unlike the displays of technology in the nineteenth and early twentieth century exhibitions, these contemporary technologies are not the focus of the displays. Thus it is neither product nor process but the effects of simulation which people wonder at and seek out.

Through these technological displays the spectacles of contemporary exhibitions are of a different kind from those of previous decades. The display of the exotic produced a sense of self in the viewer through an exaggeration of difference achieved through decontextualization and lack of information. The exotic has been replaced by the proximity of simulated experience. World fairs used to display the exotic alongside the technological to convince people of the necessity of imperial economies for the general progress of mankind (Rydell 1984). Technological possibilities were associated with national potentials and agendas, themselves objectified in the racial hierarchies on display. Today's technologies generate effects apparently without regard for cultural or racial difference. Thus, while spectacle always provoked emotion and allowed the viewer to experience vicariously without responsibility or involvement, the spectacle of the Expo'92 suggests a new chapter in the narrative which tells of human liberation through technology.[7] But the myth of equal access hides or displaces the ways in which all have equal access to what are, for some, only images – a range of choices or options which themselves reinscribe hierarchies of value and reproduce the differences of class and race. For not all can produce image to the same effect, parody is not available to all participants, not all are able convincingly to conflate image with life itself.

THE INFORMATICS OF DOMINATION

This use of simulation technology within Expo revealed its own rather sinister politics. As Haraway has written, 'We are living through a movement from an organic, industrial society to a polymorphous, information system – from all work to all play, a deadly game' (Haraway 1991: 161).

It was apparent in the Expo that not all nations were playing the same game, not everyone had moved from identities to networks, and it was the less powerful nations which were still playing within the earlier frame of reference. In Haraway's analysis, representation, bourgeois realism and white capitalist patriarchy are contrasted with simulation, postmodernist science fiction and the informatics of domination (Haraway 1991: 161–2). The latter phrase refers to the restructuring effects of technological innovations on social relations: labour relations, gender relations, representational practices. These may reproduce existing social relations but in so doing they also change both their value and their visibility. Computerized technologies make information a political quality[8] and it is the political effects to which I now turn.

The difference between the exhibits of the African Plaza and the high-tech displays of Spain and Fujitsu could be seen as the difference between representation and simulation, between shops and spectacle, material goods and ephemeral images. There was no hyper-reality in the African Plaza, the representational techniques were stunningly literal. Many national pavilions operated basically as souvenir stalls. Within the African Plaza the objects on sale were barely distinguishable from one nation to the next, wooden animals and printed cloth being the most common. Expo organizers had had to put considerable pressure on the Nigerian Government to get them to bring their exhibit from the Lagos museum, and this 'high culture' was not displayed in Nigeria's allocated national space, but apart as a separate concern. Nigeria's pavilion was also dedicated to selling local crafts and to low-tech displays of development projects. Many of the African nations had wanted to show themselves to the world by bringing fresh samples of their produce. Senegal had wanted to display fresh fish, many other countries had wanted to bring peanuts, palm oil, corn. In their place they tended to display packaged products, soap powder, beer. There were very few videos and those there were appeared on single television monitors rather than the banked monitors that converted the single image into spectacle in other venues. Displays of modernization projects were done through photographs, designers' plans and maps.

The African organizers were quite explicit about their motives for being at Expo and in their explanations they revealed an understanding that separated culture from business: 'Expo is not only about culture', they claimed. As far as the more powerful participants were concerned, this was of course an inappropriate assessment. Expo was exclusively about culture, but culture as commodity which the technologies of simulation could now generate and market without concern for relationships of production and reproduction.

Thus, despite the fact that Europe was so clearly presented as occupying a space at the centre of the world, we are not dealing with a simple metropole/colony opposition as was the case with the earlier world fairs. In these events the relationships of colonial production were central to the exhibits, and not only in terms of the international division of labour underlying industrial capitalism. The colony also provided the metropole with exotic peoples and goods which, once displayed, constituted the spectacle through which the metropole could witness its own control, and marvel at the 'other'. In Expo'92 the metropole produced intrinsic spectacle, in many cases from within its own former colonies, as for example in the cases of Venezuela or Mexico, which could now be assimilated as simply further perspectives, more difference.

Within this scenario, images of technological progress were used by participants to make connections between the particular and the universal. In this, Expo'92 continued the tradition of previous world fairs. But technological innovation has had effects and in terms of world fairs the difference it has made is linked to the ability of electronic technology to render social relations invisible. Technology as a link to the universal has always been treated as culturally neutral, as 'culture without culture' (Haraway n.d.). Haraway's concept of the informatics of domination draws our attention to the power relations that operate through these apparently culture-free zones, and reminds us of the political effects of the division of labour in which some emerge as technologically (not culturally) more advanced than others. This techno-culture denies culture and concerns itself instead with ownership. It is through the ownership of knowledge that categories of cultural distinction are created in the otherwise bland environment of Expo's homogenized cultural forms. There are thus strong resonances here with the ways in which branding operates as a way of securing market visibility through the ownership of essence. Thus, while universal exhibitions are concerned to display the overwhelming reality of technology itself, the human narratives to which these technologies are harnessed have changed. So we no longer find an unambiguous commitment to the relationship between technological development and human liberation, let alone the prospective unity of all knowledges which, according to Lyotard (1984) characterize modernist narratives on technology. The (postmodern) technical and commerical aims of optimal performance are more visible.

The mechanical age of reproduction produced objects, and their display was about their control. In this sense the world fairs operated much like museums, displaying 'the peculiar preoccupation of modern Western societies with mastering "objects of knowledge", and then publicly commemorating the victory by putting them on show' (Jordanova 1989: 40). As Rydell (1984) has argued, world fairs were about the dissemination of ideas which had direct bearing on the status of the nation state. Scientific paradigms, the emphasis on classification, evolution and racial and cultural hierarchies, were produced for popular consumption in the categorization and display of people and objects. The new communications technologies produce sensations. The emphasis is no longer exclusively on categorization as the concern is no longer to display people and objects. In this paradigm the nation is superseded and exists only as a presence made visible through the workings of invisible networks of power, like a hologram or laser image. These two possibilities for conceptualizing the nation co-exist at the Expo.

This material on the world fairs can give us one answer to the question 'What does global culture look like?'[9] As practice, global culture has become a visible struggle to produce relationships that still preserve the integrity of entities which we know as nation states. The kind of 'culture' that can achieve this effect of highly commensurable difference is a commodified object not far removed from our familiar western social scientific concept of the construct. As discussed in Chapter 2, the notion of the cultural construct is one that celebrates multiplicity; perspectives can always be added and the model is thus highly productive in an environment in which both specificity and connectedness are valued. My argument is that microelectronic technologies have enabled the development of this kind of culture which in turn fuels and is fuelled by the individualism of global capitalism.

Global culture in the Universal Exposition of 1992 did not look the same as it did in the Great Exhibition of 1851, despite the fact that many other aspects of these institutions of display have remained very stable. Culture is now not simply something to acquire but also something to experience, something to consume on the spot. It is no longer displays of goods that produce visible hierarchies of value.

The ironic commentaries on the fairs themselves, which always existed, but which were previously a critical reaction to the fairs articulated from the outside, are now integrated as further perspectives. Audiences are encouraged to interpret and make national cultures for themselves, and new technologies thus appear to encourage greater participation and reflexivity. Yet those same technologies also produce new techniques of exclusion and control.

World fairs have always been about consumption and about commodification. I have suggested that there has been a move away from the commodification of goods to the commodification of nations and the concept of culture itself. Thus, ironically, while in the representational model technology makes culture more visible, as it enables more relationships and more history, more technology also produces less culture in the simulation model where diversity works against choice and individuation.

Chapter 5

Hybrid subjects: citizens as consumers

Restoration of the origin, the task of genetic hygiene, is achieved in Carl Akeley's African Hall by an art that began for him in the 1880s with the crude stuffing of P. T. Barnum's elephant, Jumbo, who had been run down by a railroad train, the emblem of the Industrial Revolution. The end of his task came in the 1920s, with his exquisite mounting of the Giant of Karisimbi, the lone silverback male gorilla that dominates the diorama depicting the site of Akeley's own grave in the mountainous rain forest of the Congo, today's Zaire. So that it could inhabit Akeley's monument to the purity of nature, this gorilla was killed in 1921, the same year the Museum hosted the Second International Congress of Eugenics. From the dead body of the primate, Akeley crafted something finer than the living organism; he achieved its true end, a new genesis. Decadence – the threat of the city, civilization, machine – was stayed in the politics of eugenics and the art of taxidermy. And the Museum fulfilled its scientific purpose of conservation, of preservation, of the production of permanence. Life was transfigured in the principal civic arena of Western political theory – the natural body of man.

(Haraway 1989: 26–7)

Haraway's famous analysis of the displays mounted by the taxidermist Akeley in New York's Museum of Natural History suggests the ways in which museum exhibits were used to produce a sense of permanence in a changing world. In these exhibits it was particularly pure genetic origins that the museum sought to display, indeed create. Akeley's dioramas were better than the real thing, they were nature not simply conserved and preserved but purified, decontextualized and re-produced for public contemplation. The social processes on which Haraway's analysis depends are complex. There is Akeley, an individual with particular aims, obsessions, and possibilities afforded him by contemporary understandings of race, class and gender. The producer of an exhibit necessarily engages with the preoccupations, desires and expectations of his time, but he does not work alone. There are the people with whom he works, in this case rendered invisible in the final exhibit, and there is the institution that sponsors and contextualizes the exhibit. This public institution, a state body using public funds, seeks to educate and inspire moral responses in a visiting public. And finally there is this public, the citizen, the consumer, the site at which the exhibit will or will not take effect.

Haraway's essay brilliantly reveals the complex agendas of the New York Museum from the 1890s to the 1930s, with its exhibitions designed to produce displays of permanence in nature, its interest in eugenics and the promotion of racial purity and its dedication to the task of conservation for the purpose of knowing and ordering reality. Her contribution was to show the ways in which these agendas were closely inter-related both in purpose, promoting particular images of stability in times of extraordinary change, and in their use of the aesthetic of realism as the means by which such effects are produced.[1]

My interest in this chapter is to look at how the agendas of the contemporary universal exhibition are received by the visiting public. Haraway's essay suggests that a museum visitor is necessarily caught up in the complex ideological possibilities on show but she does not dwell on how these visitors made sense of what was laid before them. To ask these questions about the contemporary universal exhibition is to bring together some of the concerns addressed in Chapters 3 and 4. In Chapter 3 I argued that the universal exhibition operates in similar ways to other national institutions of display, as a technology of nationhood, providing narrative possibilities for the imagination of national cultures. The possibility of the nation state is promoted through the display of images which invoke stability, continuity and the purity of origins in a world of change and uncertainty. Ideas of evolutionary progress and hierarchical difference sustain this relationship between movement and stasis. However, as discussed in Chapter 4, the universal exhibition is increasingly involved in promoting the interests of international capital, interests which frequently run counter to those of the nation state. Here the values are choice, desire, individuality and the challenge to generate difference in a world of increasing congruity. A focus on the practice of visitors to the Expo site might help us to understand some of the ways in which these two apparently contradictory agendas co-exist in this exhibition space. Or is it the case, as Mitchell has claimed (1988: 162), that to become a citizen of an exhibitional world is to become a consumer of commodities and meanings?

These questions also enable me to return more explicitly to the relationship between cultural theory and ethnographic observation. Cultural theorists are interested in consumption and in the relationship between consumers and citizens, as the nation state becomes more explicitly a provider of services for the citizen/consumer. My interest is thus to juxtapose my observations of the cultural practice of visiting the Expo'92 with the abstract discussions of consumption by cultural theorists such as Baudrillard, Lyotard and de Certeau. The use of this literature provides another focal point for discussion – the role of the realist aesthetic in contemporary exhibitions.

It was the realist aesthetic, Haraway argued, that most appropriately enabled the expression of the holism and organicism of the American Museum of Natural History (Haraway 1989). It was also the realism which exercised a seductive power over visitors offering them a sense of unmediated vision,[2] and successfully erased alternative realities – disorders, impurities, loss. Writers such as Baudrillard and Lyotard are fascinated by the destabilization of reality that the conditions of contemporary capitalism provoke. The image of coherence is shattered by the promotion and proliferation of choice, and the subjectivity of the consumer is one of the effects of such a shattering. Haraway's analysis referred to the beginning of this century, Baudrillard and Lyotard's to its end. The Expo'92 bridged these two moments, its displays played with both the real and the hyper-real. The majority of the national exhibitors used realist techniques to build up their presentations of the nation state and to promote the possibilities and promises of modernization and technological evolution. Yet, this realism was also openly reflected upon and alternatives were offered. Some exhibitors openly invited personal interpretation. If, as Lyotard has argued, realism operates 'to preserve various consciousness from doubt', the Expo'92 was also interested in the provocation of such doubts and indeed as a manifestation of contemporary capitalism the institution could perhaps not do otherwise:

> [C]apitalism inherently possesses the power to derealise familiar objects, social roles, and institutions to such a degree that the so called realistic representations can no longer evoke reality except as nostalgia or mockery, as an occasion for suffering rather than for satisfaction. Classicism seems to be ruled out in a world in which reality is so destabilised that it offers no occasion for experience but one for ratings and experimentation.
>
> (Lyotard 1984: 143)

These apparently contradictory aesthetics of display suggest that the Expo visitors were construed and constituted as simultaneously modern coherent subjects (responding to the power of the realist aesthetic, invited to identify with a nation, region or continent), and postmodern diffuse consumers (responding to the choices laid before them, invited to enjoy difference and to satisfy personal desires). A visit to the Expo thus becomes a particular kind of cultural practice with implications for the ways in which we might theorize consumption in the late twentieth century.

Museums have long been used by nation states as a way of producing citizens and promoting the values of democracy.[3] The narratives which these institutions offered to visitors,[4] the visions of order of the type analyzed by Haraway, were offered as a public service. While particular histories, beliefs and identities were presented as matters-of-fact, rather than as matters-of-interest, visitors were invited to identify with the producers of these narratives, who were after all simply fellow citizens:

> To identify with power, to see it as, if not directly theirs, then indirectly so, a force regulated and channelled by society's ruling groups but for the good of all: this was the rhetoric of power embodied in the exhibitionary complex – a power made manifest . . . by its ability to organize and coordinate an order of things and to produce a place for the people in relation to the order.
>
> (Bennett 1988: 130)

The place which Bennett evokes is however an ambiguous one,

particularly in the universal exhibitions which were in many ways constituted by their visiting publics.[5] The exhibitions displayed power, engaged in the art of public effects,[6] made things visible and thus apparently knowable. The visitors themselves were however among the objects on display, watched from the viewing towers that have so frequently been constructed as part of exhibitionary monumental architecture. In Foucaultian terms the exhibitions actualize principles of spectacle and surveillance simultaneously, constituting the visiting public as both the subjects and objects of knowledge. Evoking the function of the Eiffel Tower at the 1889 Paris Exposition, Bennett argues:

> To see and be seen, to survey yet always be under surveillance, the object of an unknown but controlling look: in these ways, as micro-worlds rendered constantly visible to themselves, expositions realized some of the ideals of panopticism in transforming the crowd into a constantly surveyed, self-watching, self-regulating, and, as the historical record suggests, consistently orderly public – a society watching over itself.
>
> (Bennett 1988: 133)

Thus it is not just the distinction between citizens and consumers, between the interests of the nation state and of capital, that lie at the heart of the universal exhibition, but also a politics of reflexivity which invites visitors to question what they see while simultaneously ordering their responses. These are the dynamics which are the subject of this chapter.

ON CONSUMPTION

Contemporary understandings of the nature of consumption as cultural practice are complex. Debates about the nature of commodities have tended to focus on how objects acquire value through the particular relationships in which they circulate.[7] Thus, given the diversity of such relationships, we find that consumption is variously described as 'fragmenting, homogenizing, alienating or liberating' (Silverstone and Hirsch 1992: 4). In the spirit of these discussions it is my intention to avoid treating consumption as an intrinsically oppressive activity, even though an event such as the Expo'92 might be thought to epitomize the kinds of alienated desires that have led some to characterize consumption in this way.[8]

Universal exhibitions have since the beginning operated as venues for the display of the products of mass production, for the generation of the values of distinction and the formation of bourgeois tastes and desires.[9] Indeed, as Rydell has argued, it was through the display of such products that the visiting public was encouraged to accept the politics of colonialism (Rydell 1984). Manufacturing industries required the raw materials from overseas domains to develop the possibilities of civilized living. Exotic provenance could increase the value of an object, as could its novelty or scarcity. In such displays objects were thus quite clearly constituted as social forms (Miller 1987: 11). Bennett has argued that it was always the products rather than the processes of production that were stressed in the exhibits:[10]

> After 1851, world fairs were to function less as vehicles for the technical education of the working classes than as instruments for their stupefaction before the reified products of their own labor, 'places of pilgrimage,' as Benjamin put it, 'to the fetish Commodity.'[11]
>
> (Bennett 1988: 145)

Commodities are most generally thought of as manufactured goods, the products of the capitalist mode of production. Distinguished by its use value for others, a commodity is an object intended for exchange and furthermore an object in which exchangeability is its most socially relevant feature (Appadurai 1986: 13). A key aspect to the understanding of any commodity circulation is thus the way in which value is attributed. As Appadurai has argued (after Marx and Simmel), exchange is the source of value for such goods, and thus the value resides in social relations and is subject to the complexities which such relations themselves entail (Appadurai 1986: 9).

However, these relations reflect back on to the objects themselves when we consider the mechanisms of demand or desire through which they hold their value. Baudrillard, for example, defines consumption in terms of the workings of economies of desire. He finds that the Marxist focus on production only offers limited understanding of the nature of modern commodities and of consumption as activity, an activity which engages cultural systems in a very general way:

> Consumption is not a passive mode of assimilation and appro-

priation which we can oppose to an active mode of production, in order to bring to bear naïve concepts of action (and alienation). From the outset, we must clearly state that consumption is an active mode of relations (not only to objects, but to the collectivity and to the world), a systematic mode of activity and a global response on which our whole cultural system is founded.

(Baudrillard 1968: 21)

Economies of desire are fields of symbolic action. Consumer goods are 'objects made more or less desirable by the role they play in a symbolic system' (Gell 1986: 110). In the terms of these approaches to consumption, it can be seen that both consumers and commodities (the objects of consumption) are attributed a degree of agency. However, Baudrillard's contribution has been to go beyond Marx's observation that commodities like persons have social lives, to ask how it is that consumer objects have their effect. One of the important arguments on the processes of consumption at the Expo'92 will centre on the way that the fetishization of commodities has now crucially come to include the realm of 'experience' and thus, while a focus on consumption is a focus on the circulation of material objects, included among these are the material traces of experience itself.

When we look at what has been written on the consumption of packaged culture, there are two key positions which emerge in the literature and which can be characterized by the writings of Baudrillard and de Certeau.[12] I have chosen these positions because they appear, on the surface, to articulate a distinction between the textual and the interactional approaches which were the subject of discussion in Chapter 2.

Baudrillard is interested in the semiotics of value, the systems of difference through which objects acquire value, and in which subjects are motivated to consume:

Consumption is neither a material practice, nor a phenomenology of 'affluence'. It is not defined by the food we eat, the clothes we wear, the car we drive, nor by the visual and oral substance of images and messages, but in the organization of all this as signifying substance. Consumption is the virtual totality of all objects and messages presently constituted in a more or less coherent discourse. Consumption, in so far as it is meaningful, is a systematic act of the manipulation of signs.

(Baudrillard 1968: 21–2)

To understand consumption in these terms is to look at how objects are consumed not in their materiality but in their difference (Baudrillard 1968: 22).

The American Spirit Home

One of the exhibits on show at the United States pavilion was the American Spirit Home. Visitors were invited to walk around a modern American home, which was furnished and available for view in much the same way as a show home on a new estate. Its principal sponsor was the American Plywood Association, an organization that wanted to promote the use of wood products and had chosen the presentation of a house as a suggestive and appealing example. The aims were stated quite explicitly in its publicity material:

Expo'92 provides a unique opportunity for the American Plywood Association to expose hundreds of thousands of European consumers to modern American-style wood homes. Our primary goal is to create and expand markets for our members' products. Those products are not houses. They are structural wood panels and engineered wood products such as glued laminated beams. However, these products are used extensively in buildings constructed of wood. So, while we may not be selling houses, we are certainly promoting the concept of wood housing. Plus, it is these same structural wood products that enable homes with spacious design and amenities like the American Spirit to be available to European markets today.

However, despite these intentions, which I found hidden away among the details of the corporate sponsors of the United States Pavilion and which were thus unlikely to have been read by the majority of visitors, the exhibit was primarily visited as a home and it was the home that operated as the product on display. Indeed, the American Spirit Home had been featured in the *Better Homes and Gardens* magazine and was thus quite evidently a product as much on offer to the American people as to foreign viewers. This possibility must also have been appreciated by the many subsidiary corporate sponsors set out in a leaflet which attributed not just the building materials but also the electrical appliances, the fireplaces and countertops, the doors, the air conditioning, plumbing fixtures and fittings, even the china.[13]

Some visitors at least viewed the object in this light and their interpretation was one which led them to see the presence of this house as offensive. As I followed round the marked pathway, looking into the rooms from behind the cordon (in this respect it was more reminiscent of stately homes than show homes), I overheard the Spanish couple in front of me expressing their disdain for the exhibit. Who did the Americans think they were? What kind of houses did they think the Spaniards lived in? Did they think that they had not seen inside toilets or comfortable sitting rooms before? It was totally lost on them, as it was on me at that stage, that the point of the exhibit was the display of new and innovative wood products. They consumed this object in terms of its relationship to other houses with which they were already familiar. Because of their focus on its interior decoration and the facilities such as the indoor toilet which it appeared to be promoting, this house could only be rendered significant to these visitors as an example of American prejudice towards a Spanish public whom it appeared to be intending to educate in the possibilities of a civilized life-style.

Both Baudrillard (Poster 1988) and de Certeau (1984) stress the dynamic and experiential nature of consumption, both are interested in the ways in which artefacts are pressed into the enactment of already-existing social relationships.[14] However, while Baudrillard's interest is in the processes of signification which a consumer can only challenge through silence, that is through a refusal to engage,[15] de Certeau is interested in the ways in which consumers make opportunities from the meanings that are presented to them. His emphasis on the practices of everyday life emphasizes the ways in which people continually resignify the meanings that their social environment affords them. Thus, presented with the American Spirit Home, Baudrillard would be likely to be interested in the relationships that this house signifies, evokes and ultimately substitutes, the ways in which its display provokes a desire for a life-style that is simulated rather than represented: it never was real and it can thus never be achieved, although it can be desired. This focus does help to explain why it was that the Spanish couple did not relate to the house as an advertisement for innovative wood products.

De Certeau, on the other hand, alerts us to the ways in which the intentions of the American Plywood Association will inevitably be subverted by the active engagement of the consumers with their product. In the case I have described, the Spanish visitors turned this exhibit into an opportunity to voice a criticism of what they perceived to be a statement of cultural superiority. The Expo site, overdetermined in terms of its message-bearing capacity, was of course ripe for the resignifying practices which interest de Certeau.

True to the reflexive capacity of this exhibition, many of these resignifying practices were noticed and discussed in the press, and later represented in the post-exhibition display, 'Memories of the Expo'. One of the most visible ways in which visitors manipulated the Expo site to conform to the requirements of their everyday lives as visitors, was in their appropriation of the fountains, waterfalls and pools. Water was a central feature of the Expo site, with clear symbolic and practical functions:

> Most visitors will have read up about Seville: they will know all about the Giralda Tower, the patios of the Reales Alcazares Palace, and about how hot the city gets at the height of summer. The Universal Exposition has been designed so that temperatures are lowered, using age-old Arab skills in combination with state-of-the-art technology. Water plays a vital role: there is a total area of 200,000 m² of water within the Site, brought in from the Guadalquivir to feed the Lake of Spain and its waterways. Some 50,000 m of shade are cast by leafy pergolas; and 25,000 trees and 300,000 shrubs and bushes have been planted. All these natural cooling elements have been combined with bioclimatic technology. The twelve towers of the Avenue of Europe give off micronised water, and the moisture in the atmosphere is increased still further by the bioclimatic Sphere on Polar Avenue. And it is easy to escape the blinding glare of the summer sun in the Site's air-conditioned Pavilions and indoor restaurants.
>
> (Expo'92 Official Guide: 30–2)

The Expo organizers had attempted to create a micro-climate to counteract the heat of the Andalucian summer, using a combination of ancient and contemporary water technologies. Thus, while substantially reducing the temperature on the site, these ornamental water courses could simultaneously evoke the delicate refinement of Spain's ancient Arabic culture. But the heat was too much. Visitors waded unceremoniously into the ornamental pools, took off their socks and shoes and paddled in the water. Escape from the heat into the pools by the weary, footsore, overheated tourists had not been envisioned, but as soon as it happened it became incorporated as another aspect of the exhibition. The 'Memories of the Expo' exhibit dwelt on the appropriation of the water by visitors, displaying photographs and taped conversations about the heat. This case exemplifies Bennett's discussion of the conjunction of spectacle and surveillance, and the ways in which the reflexivity of this event transforms reinterpretation back into spectacle, in turn held up for view. In such conditions participation of the public in the interpretation of exhibits does not easily constitute a redistribution of power, any such possibility being systematically undermined by the ways in which alternative readings of Expo narratives are simply held up as instances of consumer choice.

KNOWLEDGE AND CHOICE

Interest in the ways in which people interpreted the displays at the Expo prompted me to interview visitors. I asked what people remembered, what they had enjoyed, what they thought the event was about. The interpretative practices of consumers at an event such as the Expo ultimately defy description, and I am in no way claiming that the representations which I happened to recover were in any way typical or symptomatic. All I can do is recognize and highlight the resonances which these particular instances afford. As Ang has noted with regard to television consumption, there are no ideal consumers: 'If we take full account of this inherently tactical nature of television consumption, we must come to the conclusion that any attempt to construct positive knowledge about the "real consumer" will always be provisional, partial, fictional' (Ang 1992: 142).

One of the interesting areas of resonance was in those responses which demonstrated that the reflexive complexity of the exhibitions' producers was reproduced by those who visited the displays. This is not to say that the intentions of particular exhibits were necessarily recovered, but rather that the cultural understandings which provoked the use of particular forms and the display of particular messages were also brought to bear in the interpretative process. A typical example was the way in which visitors did not require either the exhibits or their responses to them to express a rationalizing coherence.

For example, when I asked people what they thought the Expo was about, what the exhibition was trying to achieve as an event, I was told that participants were trying to show the customs of their country, the ways of life, buildings, culture, etc. Nation states were trying to show what they had, what they produce. It was mentioned that the pavilions operate as embassies for their country, displaying its history, its products and raw materials. On reflection, however, these same people produced contrasting accounts. They stressed that it was not just about culture, but also about showing the latest technologies, about producing a modernist image, about showing how up-to-date the country was. In this sense it was about showing the best, rather than trying to show things as they were. One man went on to say that the Expo was not about representing the country at all; after all, he insisted, it was very difficult to represent a country, that was not the point.[16] Nobody would go into an exhibit and think that that was all there was to a particular country or region. He thought that the French pavilion was wonderful, really beautiful, inside it was spectacular, it showed impressive technological development. He and his wife had looked down into the mirrored video pit from the moving walkway, but he did not think that these films represented France. He had a similar view of the United States pavilion. His visit here had been very brief, but had confirmed his expectations: 'the typical, some bloke, basketball, all Yankee, everything huge, fantastic, American, baseball – not reality either!'

In their interpretations of the purpose of the displays we thus find three distinctive responses: nations show things as they are, they show the best that they have to offer, they show an image of themselves that does not conform to any particular reality. It is interesting that these distinctions reproduce quite closely Baudrillard's phases of the image:

These would be the successive phases of the image:
1 It is the reflection of a basic reality.
2 It masks and perverts a basic reality.

3 It masks the *absence* of a basic reality.
4 It bears no relation to any reality whatever: it is its own pure simulacrum.

(Baudrillard 1981: 170)

The parallelisms in these accounts will be discussed in more detail below.

To continue with the ways in which visitors did not seek to iron out the contradictions in their responses to the Expo, it was clear that while everyone I spoke to was very enthusiastic about their visit, they were also quite critical. Some people reflected on the politics of the exhibition, and expressed reservations about the benefits of such an event. In more specific terms there was general agreement that the exhibits were not worth the queues. While they might be interesting or fun they were not good enough to warrant an eight hour queue. However, I was also repeatedly told that the visit to the Expo had been a chance in a lifetime, this was not something which they would be able to do again. Indeed it was due to the perceived unique nature of the Exposition that people travelled from all over Spain to visit. The uniqueness lay in the fact that it was organized by Spain (and implicitly for Spaniards). There might be other exhibitions but not Spanish ones. In similar vein people commented on the overall impact of the exhibition. They spoke about the architecture, the massive entrance gateways, the scale of the site and the complexity of the water technologies.

This discussion of interpretative possibilities brings me back to the issue of choice and Baudrillard's understandings of consumer culture and economies of desire. If we consider the case of advertising, and the issue of branding discussed in Chapter 4, what an advertisement needs to achieve, in order to be rendered effective, is not the recovery of any literal or surface messages produced by the advertiser, but the transference of meaning from the object in question to the person of the consumer. In this respect, 'advertising codes products through symbols that differentiate them from other products, thereby fitting the object into a series. The object has its effect when it is consumed by transferring its "meaning" to the individual consumer' (Poster 1988: 2). The desire for the reality which the object simulates, becomes the consumer's desire which can never be fulfilled as there is no reality which can respond to the sense of lack that has been invoked. It is within the parameters of this understanding of the effects of messages churned out by the mass media and information technologies that Baudrillard questions the notions of choice or self-determination which de Certeau's more optimistic tactical responses imply.

A consideration of how people made their way around the Expo site illustrates these points. One of the standard fantasies in which visitors were obliged to participate was the redrawn map of the world (Figure 10). The layout of the site was designed and negotiated with particular interpretative possibilities in mind. The national and corporate participants understood that the symbolism of their relative positioning would be an aspect of their displays with which the visiting public would engage. Disputes about the layout of the site were basically attempts to pre-empt or predetermine specific interpretations.

Spain dominated this new ideal world with its commanding focal site at the head of the Avenue of Europe on the edge of the newly constructed Lake of Spain. The space it occupied was doubled by the display of its disaggregated component parts, the seventeen autonomous regions, ranged around the far shores of the lake. The pavilion of the European Community occupied a position in the centre of the European Avenue. The exhibition space was underground, not visible from the outside. What could be seen was the multicoloured tower designed to display simultaneously the flags of all the Community members in the order of their affiliation. The twelve Community countries were also literally attached to the tower by cloth awnings which spanned the walkway. Arab nations, participating in their own right for the first time at a world fair, were grouped at the eastern end of the precinct, including in their midst the most expensive pavilion of the Expo, the hand crafted (US $35 million) Moroccan palace (Figure 11).

The western end of the site was dominated by a large office-style building, the Plaza of the Americas, the subject of intense pre- Expo negotiations which well illustrate the politics involved in drawing up the final world map (Figure 12). The Expo organizers were concerned that Latin American nations should have a high profile. It was for this reason that they built this multiplex pavilion, not simply to house all those Latin American nations that wished to participate but also to secure for them a dominant position equalled only by that of Spain itself. There were, how-

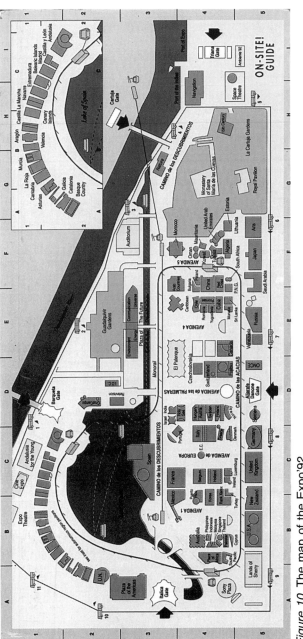

Figure 10 The map of the Expo'92
Source: The Best of Expo © 1992 by On Site Publications

Figure 11 The Moroccan pavilion
Source: Penelope Harvey

ever, unfortunate implications in this design. In the first place the pavilion *did* appear to be *integrated* into the Spanish section of the site. Furthermore, even it if were argued that the positioning could indicate an equivalence of status between the Americas and Spain, the effect was to reduce a whole continent to a single locale. Not all the Latin American nations were prepared to accept this arrangement. It was argued that they would appear as the poor relations which would give a negative image of the economies which they had come to Spain to promote. Mexico, Chile, Venezuela and Cuba opted to build pavilions at their own expense on separate sites outside the Americas building. Things were beginning to look bad for the Expo management. The building was already constructed and it seemed possible that they might not be able to fill it. Expo subsidized participation in this building. For many of the nations it was not just the venue they provided but the transport and insurance of the exhibits, and the travel and accommodation of personnel. Further temptations of privileged business agreements for the shops and restaurants which some of the nations wished to set up secured the crucial presence of Colombia, Argentina and Brazil, three nations which might have been able to finance a separate participation. It is noteworthy that throughout these negotiations the economies of Mexico and Venezuela were respected in their own right but there were fierce struggles with Cuba, which wished to remain independent despite the cost. The fact of independent survival was one of the primary messages which Cuba wished to convey. Chile was openly elitist, its Commissioner declaring in public that Chile did not wish to be associated with the Blacks and Indians inside the Plaza.

The concern of the Latin Americans about their portrayal as the poor of the Expo, was echoed in the concerns of the African nations. There were those who argued that it was worse for the Latin Americans because they could be seen to be poor, while the Africans with their North facing position, looking away from the main site on to the newly built motorway could not even be seen and therefore had less to worry about in terms of negative effect! The African nations were also housed in an Expo building, another permanent structure built with future purposes in mind, hence its somewhat alternative orientation. Unlike the Latin American states, not all African states were represented; a sample was enough to provide the world context in which to set Spain and Europe. The Expo management defended themselves from criticism with the argument that Africa was a lesser priority

Figure 12 The Plaza of the Americas
Source: Penelope Harvey

than South America, or alternatively that they had spent more
on the participation of Third World countries than any previous
Expo.

Visitors to the Expo were encouraged to choose their own viewing strategies.[17] There was no particular narrative which they were encouraged to follow, or specific links between one part of the exhibition and another which might require exhibits to be viewed in a particular order. For many people the site was initially very confusing – extensive, hot and crowded with huge queues for the most popular exhibits. Indeed many of those I talked to had started their tour by simply choosing a pavilion which had no queue. Throughout, the ethos of the active consumer was promoted and guidebooks and bulletins were published to aid visitors in their choices. This notion of choice was of course in many ways illusory. As we have seen, the layout of the site was designed to pre-empt particular interpretative possibilities. One of the reasons for the massive queues was that visits to particular pavilions were highly controlled. A set number of visitors was admitted at timed intervals. They were ushered through the audio-visual exhibits at a carefully regulated pace, their visit co-ordinated precisely with the rhythm of the spectacle which they were invited to witness. The extensive use of audio-visual materials which the visitors themselves did not control exacerbated this pattern. In fact many visitors complained to me that it was the widespread use of these audio-visuals which limited their choices of which pavilions could be visited in the time they had. One man remarked that his family had travelled 1,000 km to find that they were not able to see the pavilions that had motivated the visit. However, the ethos of choice remained, and the controlled manner in which visitors were obliged to watch the films was offset by the many interactive exhibits with which visitors could choose to engage.

Interactive exhibits have become increasingly popular in museums as curators have tried to find ways to draw the public into exhibitions while maintaining a balance between education and entertainment.[18] Public institutions which seek to actively engage in mass education have to make their material not only accessible but also attractive, and international exhibitions have always had this overtly egalitarian ethos.[19] Some have argued that the educational properties of exhibits are increasingly subordinated to their entertainment value, and that the knowledge acquired by visitors who engage with these exhibits is illusory, as is the notion that the visitor is exercising more autonomy than when presented with a more static exhibit that requires a viewer simply to look.[20] What is undeniable is that the use of interactive exhibits does lead to the viewer becoming inscribed into the exhibition in ways that highlight the fact that an exhibition visit is an embodied experience.[21] This runs counter to the traditional ethos of public museums:

> Because looking, unlike touching, does not apparently affect its object – it is not 'interactive' – the public's opportunity to gaze upon the narratives of knowledge in the museum helped to confirm a notion of knowledge as embodied in the physical world and not in human subjectivities.
>
> (Macdonald 1993a: 8)

An interesting corollary of these debates is the suggestion that viewing is a passive activity while the engagement of other senses in itself renders the process more active, the experience more valid. However, if we ask the question in another way; if we were to look, as Strathern has suggested, at the kinds of persons people make out of themselves in such interactions, we are brought up against the mimetic effects of interactive technologies, devices which compel particular responses and which amplify choices only in relation to themselves (Strathern 1992e).

Arguments on the relationship between education and diversion rely on a further epistemological distinction between pleasure and learning: 'Why educational? Why should the purpose of making exhibitions not be simply to give pleasure, to provide entertainment or diversion?' (Vergo 1989: 58). This distinction takes me back to a point that was raised in Chapter 2 concerning the distinction between my attempts to analyze and understand the workings of the Expo and other visitors' intentions simply to enjoy themselves. The point that is not addressed in this formulation is the way in which alternative domains of contextualization were drawn on in the interpretative practices of myself and certain other visitors. The distinction between pleasure and learning[22] could be used to distinguish the response of someone who attempts to engage with the exhibition by looking for meaning and formulating interpretations (as I found myself doing when I arrived), and someone who is primarily concerned with enjoying themselves. However, there was also considerable enjoyment to be had from interpretative practice, which emerges when we consider the ways in which visitors engaged with the reflexivity of the Expo exhibits.

When I talked to people about their impressions of the exhibition, 'interpretations' were not given in terms of what things meant but more in terms of how it felt to participate. Overall narratives of memories of the visits centred on the expression of emotion and the attribution of value. They talked of how beautiful things were, how gorgeous, spectacular, impressive, sensational; they mentioned the desire to see as much as possible, the pleasure of their visits, the entertainment value. And, perhaps not surprisingly, the things that afforded greatest pleasure were not the material artefacts on display but the more ephemeral visual imagery, the hyper-real rather than the mundane realities. Many people talked of their delight at watching the sound and light show which took place every night on the Lake of Spain. At the climax of this event, the water was shot upwards to form a screen onto which were projected laser-generated images of flamenco dancers who then appeared to be performing on the lake itself. I also noted the pleasure afforded by the ways in which the Expo exhibitors were able to recreate not just artefacts but environments. One couple talked about how they had found these great bars which made them feel as if they were sitting in Seville's old quarter. The same drinks were served, the same music played, even the atmosphere was reproduced. I found this somewhat ironic, given that this reproduction was at most only ten minutes' walk away from the original. Or perhaps that was not the point, these imitation bars were perhaps more friendly, more 'authentic', more real and thus more enjoyable. And the 'original' itself was another representation, evocative of former times and previous life-styles, preserved or recreated for tourists and nostalgic locals. Another similar example came up in a discussion on the exhibit of Asturias, one of Spain's autonomous regions. This was one of those pavilions that used extensive audiovisuals and models to simulate scenes through history. The visitor was engulfed in the sights and sounds of the scenes. The woman I talked to about it remarked on how she had found it so beautiful because it was so life-like. She was particularly impressed by some cows, because they looked so natural. My suggestion is that the enjoyment here was derived precisely from the unreality of these cows and the fact that despite their artificiality they so closely resembled 'the real thing'. I suspect that real cows would have been far less interesting.[23]

This disjunction between the real and the simulated was the

subject of reflexive awareness and a source of fun. Two very similar incidents illustrate this point. The first took place in the Venezuelan pavilion. Visitors had filed into the huge auditorium to watch the film, *Land of Grace*. This film, with its high resolution technology and giant screen was widely recommended as one of the more spectacular audio-visuals on display at the Expo and due to its popularity there were long queues. When people had taken their seats there was a short welcoming address and finally the hostesses announced that the film would now begin and that the 3-D glasses were under the seats. People scrabbled down to find them and there was much laughter at the realization that there were of course no glasses there at all. Some people seemed bewildered but most knew that this invitation to put on the glasses was in fact a reference to the other hugely popular audio-visual, Fujitsu's three-dimensional movie *Echoes of the Sun*. Enjoyment of this joke was entirely dependent on an 'intertexual' reference to another exhibit and an awareness of the implicit competition for popularity between exhibitors. While the majority of people did look under their seats for the glasses I would also suggest that this same majority also knew perfectly well that they were not going to see a three-dimensional movie. Another dimension to the joke was thus also that they had allowed themselves to be tricked in their search for sensation. From the point of view of the organizers the joke was a timely reminder that sensation was indeed what these visitors wanted, and the suggestion was that this sensation would indeed be delivered although not in the same form as that offered by competitors. This form of entertainment, via the invocation of contextual reference which the visitor is required to recover, was also used in the British pavilion in a very similar way. As the visitors reached the final stage of their tour, they took their seats in a theatre and were told by their British 'navigators'[24] that this show was unique among those on offer at the Expo'92 as it combined live performance with multi-media projections. Visitors were then instructed to fasten their seat-belts as the show was about to begin. Again, much scrambling for non-existent seat-belts, and laughter at what was here attributed to a British sense of humour. The reference was perhaps more pointed given that it was the Spanish Moviemax production which did require viewers to fasten themselves into the moving seats, and the majority of visitors were of course Spanish.

The pleasure associated with these interpretative practices is the pleasure afforded by the recognition of the absent referent. Possibilities of engaging in these practices depend crucially on specialized expertise. The two examples I have given here are instances in which many people could participate as the hidden referents were in fact highly salient and accessible to many people. Other 'jokes' were more subtle and take us into the realm of the relationship between reflexivity and parody. The designation of the medieval monastery as the nerve centre of the contemporary exhibition was a case in point. This building had the perfect history for a symbolic encapsulation of the event: an early haven for Columbus as he planned his journeys to the Americas, a resting place for his remains, a vestige of the industrial revolution when it was an English-owned pottery factory, evidence of industrial decline and of post-industrial regeneration, space for the reception of royalty and for the general public, for the exhibition of fifteenth century art and for a multi-media extravaganza on the fifteenth century. Today it is a national monument and a central symbol for the Expo'92, objectifying the simultaneity of the fifteenth and twenty-first centuries. In the process of course, history is flattened, the specificity of its presence erased by the contemporary show. This building is a parody in ways very similar to the parodies of the Swiss pavilion analyzed in Chapters 3 and 4. The building is taken seriously yet the layers of self-reference are such that it also stands as an exquisite example of that conflation of the simulated and the real that so fascinates Baudrillard.

Baudrillard has argued that it is now impossible to rediscover an absolute level of the real. Neither the processes of simulation nor those of the real can be isolated as each now implies the other. He claims, for example, that it would be impossible to organize a fake hold-up. If the simulation were effective it would be because the artificial could no longer be distinguished from the real, not least in terms of effects. Thus all hold-ups, hijacks and the like are now, as it were, simulation hold-ups, in the sense that they are inscribed in advance in what he refers to as the decoding and orchestration rituals of the media. They are anticipated in their mode of presentation and possible consequences. Parody is a form of presentation in which these elisions are presented for enjoyment. Thus, although the building could be understood as having had culturally and historically specific origins, and a historical narrative can be constructed in which the building is the stable referent in a changing world, its latest appropriation by the universal exhibition also leads one to question the origins of this narrative. To what extent is this building merely a symbol, a persuasive signifier for an imaginary and all too coherent history? What is the relationship between surface and depth in this building turned cultural artefact? If the many facets of its history are simultaneously visible, are we as viewers invited to view this history or are we just looking at an image of something which other media productions have prepared us to accept as history? Does not part of the pleasure of contemplating the Monastery of Santa Maria de las Cuevas lie in the simultaneous promise of proximity to authentic forms and their ultimate unattainability? We can make of it what we will. In the same way the authenticity of the Spanish bar is brought into question by the presence of the copy which does not seek to hide its artifice. Here we approach Lyotard's understanding of the postmodern but with the added claim that a recognition of these processes does itself afford pleasure:

> The postmodern would be that which, in the modern, puts forward the unpresentable in presentation itself; that which denies itself the solace of good forms, the consensus of a taste which would make it possible to share collectively the nostalgia for the unattainable; that which searches for new presentations, not in order to enjoy them but in order to impart a stronger sense of the unpresentable.
>
> (Lyotard 1984: 149)

In Lyotard's formulation the enjoyment and knowledge are distinguished. My contention is that in the context of an event such as the Expo'92, there is great pleasure to be derived from the recognition of this gap between the possibilities of presentation and the unpresentable, and the simultaneity of forms which evoke nostalgia and yet openly confuse the distinctions between the real and the copy. Furthermore, by participating knowingly in such scenarios, visitors further confound the notions of expertise to the extent that it becomes problematic to claim that knowledge is illusory.

The distinction between the Expo as an educational and as a recreational experience cannot be drawn simply in terms of whether interpretative or representational strategies are brought to bear. However, in a belief that there are ways of distinguishing superficial from more grounded understandings and that knowledges are not equally illusory, I will return to Baudrillard's theories of consumption, and to my observations of how people moved around the Expo site and the variety of ways in which they sought to objectify their experiences. These particular strategies of representation reveal that the practice of consumption, while pervasive, is not by any means definitive of the social relations of our time.

CONSUMPTION AS FRUSTRATED DESIRE

The object of consumption quite precisely is *that in which the project is 're-signed'*. This suggests that *there are no limits to consumption*. If it was that which it is naïvely taken to be, an absorption, a devouring, then we should achieve saturation. If it was a function of the order of needs, we should achieve satisfaction. But we know that this is not the case: we want to consume more and more. ... At the heart of the project from which emerges the systematic and indefinite process of consumption is a frustrated desire for totality. Object-signs are equivalent to each other in their ideality and can proliferate indefinitely: and *they must* do so in order continuously to fulfil the absence of reality. It is ultimately because consumption is founded on a *lack* that it is irrepressible.

(Baudrillard 1968: 25)

This abstract declaration on the nature of consumption is the kind of statement that annoys the anthropologists of a more empiricist bent, yet when we look at how visitors moved around the Expo site, Baudrillard's analysis (apparently ungrounded) has, at the very least, pinpointed a key aspect of people's activities, an apparent insatiability, and an urgency not usually associated with leisure. There is no doubt that the leisure activity of a visit to the Expo is extremely hard work.

By August 1992 the numbers of visitors to the Expo site were in excess of 500,000 per day. As a result there were extremely long queues to what had, by popular consent, become the principal pavilions: Canada, Fujitsu, Spain, Navigation. A wait of up to eight hours was not unusual. Some people chose to view one or two of these exhibits. There was intense competition to get to the front of the queues, people literally running across the site as soon as the gates opened in the mornings. Many others decided on an alternative strategy, to see as much as the rest of the exhibition as possible. Some, as we have seen, gave up and sat in the ornamental pools. There was, of course, no standard way of viewing exhibits, but there were a noticeable number of people who moved through the pavilions without really looking at anything. They went to get a general idea and to accumulate experience in a quantifiable way.

In keeping with the idea of a world tour, visitors could acquire an Expo passport. All pavilions had a stamp, usually at the exit to the exhibit and visitors could thus collect the material evidence of having visited each nation. Those who passed through the exhibits with great speed were often simply looking for the place where they could get their passports stamped. Each pavilion also had PINs, small identity brooches, sometimes for sale, but more usually given away to special visitors. These were the more valued collectibles of a pavilion visit, they signified a privileged relationship, and were traded among Expo personnel. The most interesting feature of these two forms of representing the fact of having been to a particular pavilion was that for many people the accumulation of these signs was more important than the content of the exhibit itself. In some cases, as I have suggested, this was manifested in the way in which people rushed through the exhibitions, not stopping to read labels or look at the items on display. In other more extreme cases people collected stamps and PINS from pavilions that they had not even visited. A pavilion hostess told me that everyday they found passports that visitors had dropped or mislaid. They would keep them for two or three days but after that they were used to placate distraught visitors whose 'accumulated experiences' had vanished as it were on the loss of their passport. These visitors would express great excitement if the new passport already had a significant number of stamps. The visiting strategy would then take off from the recorded visits of the previous owner – after all there would be no point in revisiting pavilions from which a stamp had already been given. Thus, while in the non-Expo world, a passport marks the identity of a person and records his or her movements across international boundaries, at the Expo passports recorded movements but the movements were transferable from one person to another. Experience was not person specific, the only continuity was the importance of accumulation, the drive towards totality.

Used in this way the passports were pure simulacra, not simply an imitation of the way in which passports operate outside the Expo, but a play with experience that cannot be captured if treated simply as representational practice. If, however, it is acknowledged that there was pleasure to be derived from the collection of signifiers with or without their concomitant referents, then we are perhaps discussing a very concrete instance of the relationships of consumption described by Baudrillard, in which objects are consumed not in their materiality but in their difference, in the evocation or simulation of relationships and experiences where reality is less important than signification.

The use of photography and video was also interesting in this respect. Material evidence of the Expo visits was collected by many in this way. It was the use of video which I found particularly remarkable in the light of the present discussion. Again I found that people were using camcorders to record things which they themselves had not experienced. One very common way in which this occurred was the use of the camcorder as an extension of the body, as an eye that could see beyond what was physically possible for the camera operator at the time. This happened particularly when there were large crowds watching events in the street. People would hold their cameras up above their heads, to capture a scene which they could not otherwise have observed. Although I was unable to follow through the ways in which the images thus generated were used by visitors, it is noteworthy that the technique affords a possibility for generating visual memories of events which were never in fact witnessed, or for deferring 'experience' until the event could be relived in the comfort of one's own home. Even more remarkable in this respect was the use of camcorders inside the major movie theatres.

Although their use was prohibited, small red lights among the shadowy figures in the darkened auditoriums indicated that some people were filming the films. What was remarkable about this activity was the way in which, through their use of the camcorders, people were making copies of images which could not be reproduced due to their technological specificity. The reason these cinematic experiences were so popular was because of the sensations evoked by their scale. The massive screens and the high-resolution film technologies produced the hyper-realism that led viewers to feel as if they were themselves inhabiting the scenes which the screen images depicted. The thrill of the Fujitsu theatre was not just the size but also the three dimensions, the spherical auditorium and the wrap-around sound that made the viewer feel even more literally immersed in the images. A camcorder cannot reproduce these effects, the three-dimensional film would have been reduced to its two synchronic images, the scale and sound effects would also disappear. Proximity to the screen would also have made it impossible to capture the whole image at once. Again the only purpose such records could serve would be as material traces of having been there.

My final observation of these ways of collecting and accumulating the experience of the pavilions concerns the purchase of souvenirs. Most of the pavilions sold consumer goods identified with the particular nation state. There were also, as I indicated earlier, maps, plans, postcards, guidebooks, further information or privileged perspectives on a particular site. The Expo itself as event was objectified in the person of a cartoon figure, Curro – reproduced in many forms from plastic models, to cups and T-shirts (Figure 13). There were also Expo employees who appeared from time to time as the cartoon character Curro, wearing an inflatable suit, to zoom around the Expo lake on a jet ski or perform some other high-profile promotional activity. For the more discerning there were numerous facsimiles of books concerned with events in 1492 – authenticated copies of rare forms. I would suggest that these goods were not purchased for their use value, despite the fact that they often had such value, but in similar ways to the Benetton products discussed in Chapter 4, these objects were distinctive because of their association with the Expo site. Expo had become a brand which could market objects, any object, through an evocation of a future need for a memory of the Expo visit itself, however mediated that memory might be.

There was a shop at the exit to the Israeli pavilion. I cannot remember well the items on sale here, except for a carton of bookmarks which stood near the till. As I was casting an eye over what was on sale I noticed someone walk over and help themselves to one of these. Others immediately followed until several dozen had been carried away. The shop assistant, who noticed too late what was happening, was horrified. These items were for sale and from her point of view, they had been blatantly

Figure 13 Curro, the official Expo'92 mascot
Source: Penelope Harvey

stolen. But it could also be argued that the visitors were simply collecting, in almost automatic fashion, another memento. I doubt that many of them even remarked that it was a bookmark, let alone a stolen one. Many pavilions had leaflets, paper mementos which visitors collected as they left – the Israeli bookmarks were another souvenir, an object to commemorate a visit. The form of this object was not expected to refer to the visit itself, but there was a strong expectation that some objective form would be acquired and saved.

It is in the light of these practices that we can talk of the commodification of experience at the Expo.[25] Macdonald has remarked of museums that the move from a conceptualization of the museum as an élite institution with an educational purpose to the more entrepreneurial approach with a focus on entertainment has led to the commodification of the museum visit (Macdonald 1992b: 14). Museums also seek to promote themselves as brands in order to give rise to sales of objects which signify no more than the fact that the museum was visited and that the values with which the particular institution is associated might now in some way adhere to the person who carries its material trace.

If such is the nature of consumption how might we now conceptualize experience and to what extent does the conflation of simulation and representation integral to the experience of an event such as the Expo affect the ways in which we conceptualize relationships?

EXPERIENCE AND MODERNITY

The role of the self in the making of knowledge is a central issue in accounts of modernity and one related to our present concerns. As Foucault has argued, observation and the role of the observing subject was crucial to the emergence of modern European society,[26] as was the idea that society or the world could be conceptualized as a coherent image.[27] The distinctive feature of visual modernity concerns the rooting of the observer in the mobile body, and by extension knowledge became intrinsically linked to personal experience.[28] As Poole has noted on the science of Humboldt, the naturalist/explorer of South America:

[B]ecause the understanding of place was so intimately tied to the disciplined sensuous responses of the traveller who reacts to a particular view or scene, it would henceforth be necessary to ground theory in the physical experience of 'having been there'.

(Poole 1996: 101)

Thus, while it is often assumed that the development of the scientific method required the ruthless erasure of self in the interests of objective observation, those who have analyzed the practices of knowledge formulation have found that late nineteenth and early twentieth century scientists were frequently fascinated by the role they themselves played in the making of knowledge.[29]

Knowledge as image, being there to personally experience the sight, and observing the conditions of one's own observation; these are not the exclusive domains of a postmodernist, reflexive approach to knowledge. Indeed they were operating several centuries ago. Shapin and Schaffer express most eloquently how conventions of witnessing were vital to the production of knowledge in the mid-seventeenth century:

Boyle proposed that matters of fact be established by the aggregation of individuals' *beliefs*. Members of an intellectual collective had mutually to assure themselves and others that belief in an empirical experience was warranted. Matters of fact were the outcome of the process of having an empirical experience, warranting it to oneself, and assuring others that grounds for their belief were adequate. In that process a multiplication of the witnessing experience was fundamental. An experience, even of a rigidly controlled experimental performance, that one man alone witnessed was not adequate to make a matter of fact. If that experience could be extended to many, and in principle to all men, then the result could be constituted as a matter of fact. In this way, the matter of fact is to be seen as both an epistemological and a social category. The foundational item of experimental knowledge, and of what counted as properly grounded knowledge generally, was an artefact of communication and whatever social forms were deemed necessary to sustain and enhance communication.

(Shapin and Schaffer 1985: 25)

The conventions and technologies through which knowledge

emerges in this account, depend crucially not simply on multiple witnessing, but on expert witnessing. Witnesses had to have credible, valid, moral judgements. The communicative practices through which knowledges emerged were exclusive and specialized. What is interesting about the production of knowledge over three centuries later, on a site such as the Expo, is that expertise is now in the public domain in a rather different way. However, the result is not primarily a democratization of knowledge, but rather a devaluing of what can be known. The universal exhibition thus presents an encyclopaedic array of objects and technological effects to a wide audience of witnesses, and while some matters of fact are doubtless established in this process, effects are not controlled in the ways that interested scientists such as Boyle and Hobbes, because interpretations are not controlled. This suggests that the matters of fact that the Expo establishes are not of a similar order of knowledge. Jordanova has gone so far as to argue that knowledge acquired in museums has the quality of fantasy because the generation of knowledge from the visual experience is only possible through an imaginative process (Jordanova 1989). Similarly Stewart argues most elegantly that the techniques of gigantism and miniaturization also play their part in distancing the visitor from the object of knowledge while simulating the sensation of proximity:

> The miniature allows us only visual access to surface and texture; it does not allow movement through space. Inversely, the gigantic envelops us, but is inaccessible to lived experience. Both modes of exaggeration tend toward abstraction in proportion to the degree of exaggeration they allow.
>
> (Stewart 1993: 102)

What does appear to be particular to contemporary knowledge practices is the way in which the realist aesthetic has become relatively less important, the establishment of the idea that observation in itself does not necessarily lead to a firmer grip on reality but only to the generation of further perspectives, and the notion that the kinds of experiences that generate new knowledges need not be real but are often more usefully simulated. While representational practices which treated the world as exhibition always did lead to an endless deferral of reality, such deferral is now explicit and on show. The promise of the new information technologies is, after all, precisely that we will no longer have to be there to know. Experience and interaction are still important but the world as exhibition has itself produced the possibility of the world as image, to the extent that simulated form can now be explicitly offered as a more reliable substitute for 'natural' form. In his essay on physiognomic aspects of visual worlds, Taussig (1993: 19–32), attributes a revolutionary potential to mimetic modes of perception, ways of knowing that require bodily involvement. Similarly in her discussion of Walter Benjamin's interest in mimetic cognition, Buck-Morss outlines the ways in which knowledges derived from interactive engagement with the world can be contrasted to bourgeois socialization in which these ways of knowing are suppressed and knowledge is gained by looking without touching, by passive reception rather than active engagement (Buck-Morss 1991: 263–70). In these discussions considerable importance is attributed to film as a mimetic technology. Film, through its techniques of altering the experience of space and time, opens up possibilities for reflexivity. I cite Taussig, citing Virilio, citing Vertov, the Russian cinematographer:

> I am the camera's eye. I am the machine which shows you the world as I alone see it. Starting from today, I am forever free of human immobility. I am in perpetual movement. I approach and draw away from things – I crawl under them – I climb on them – I am on the head of a galloping horse – I burst at full speed into a crowd – I run before running soldiers – I throw myself down on my back – I rise up with aeroplanes – I fall and I fly at one with the bodies falling or rising through the air.
>
> (Taussig 1993: 27)[30]

Virilio's interest is in the relationship between particular types of visualization and capacities for destruction. However, the passage reminds me of the sensuous connections which the Expo films established, the ways in which the cameras allowed viewers to shoot the rapids, hang-glide, parachute, sit on the heads of horses, rise with aeroplanes, etc. For Benjamin and Buck-Morss, as for many theorists of learning,[31] there is an important difference between cognitive reception via contemplation and that which results from action. But where do we situate action in a world of simulated experience, in which viewers can remain passive despite their engagement in tactile knowing? The contrast makes clear that what are lost in such simulations are the social relations in and through which original forms were previously experienced. This is Baudrillard's dilemma:

> When the hierarchical organization of space that privileges the eye and vision, this perspective simulation – for it is merely a simulacrum – disintegrates, something else emerges; this we express as a kind of *touch*, for lack of a better term, a tactile hyperpresence of things, 'as if we could grasp them'. But this tactile fantasy has nothing to do with our sense of touch: it is a metaphor for 'seizure', the annihilation of the scene and space of representation. As a result, this seizure rebounds on the surrounding world we call 'real', revealing to us that 'reality' is nothing but a staged world, objectified according to rules of depth, that is to say the principle upon which paintings, sculptures, and the architecture of a period are defined, but only a principle; a simulacrum which the experimental hyper-simulation of the trompe-l'oeil undermines.
>
> (Baudrillard 1979: 156)

Much of what I have described of the use of film technologies at the Expo'92 is, I would suggest, captured by Baudrillard's formulation. Similarly in those patterns of consumption which I have discussed, we can see the ways in which objects routinely come to substitute for relations and even for other objects. The Peruvians, in an attempt to teach people something they did not already know, decided to focus on pre-Inca rather than Inca artefacts in their exhibit. The recently discovered tomb of the Señor de Sispan, a pre-Inca ethnic lord, provided a perfect centre-piece for such an exhibit. For reasons of security and to allow the public greater access to the ancient treasures, copies were made. The originals were on display in reinforced glass cabinets which ran along the sides of the exhibit space. In the centre of the room were larger-than-life-size models of figures 'radiantly attired' in the copies, which people could approach and even touch. It was the copies which engaged people's attention, the originals were largely ignored. They were not hidden, the pretence was overt. It was simply that the originals were less relevant to the kinds of understandings which people expected and pursued in an event of this kind. It could be argued that in some sense the originals themselves were reflections of the copies.

The revelation of staged realities at the Expo'92 was most vividly addressed in the use of mirrors. The vertigo-inducing experience of the French pavilion has already been referred to, as has the mirror in the Irish pavilion which enabled viewers to address the illogical possibility of seeing themselves in former times. Mirrored video pits changed the nature of images by their endless reproduction, as did mirrors placed so that visitors could watch their own images infinitely receding into a distant space that did not appear to be really there. One of my favourite and most straightforward memories of the play with mirrors returns me to the camcorder: a man stood on his own at the bar in the German pavilion, studiously videoing himself in the mirror, capturing perhaps the experience of being there in the late twentieth century.[32]

Before concluding this chapter, however, it is most important to stress that the previous examples are themselves partial accounts. They are interpretative possibilities which interest me, and which can become adequate descriptions when framed in particular theoretical contexts. Mimetic modes of perception might, contrary to Baudrillard's expectation, open up spaces for critical reflection as Taussig, Buck-Morss and others have suggested. Most visitors were also engaged with a 'real world', presented to them in what appeared and were taken as straightforward realist images. It was this approach which allowed them to make the political critique of the Expo exhibits that were frequently voiced. For example, when I asked one man what had most impressed him, he replied that it was the exhibits of Morocco and South Africa. He said that what had impressed him were the disjunctions between the displays and what he knew to be the social realities of these nation states.

This visitor himself worked with marble and he was thus very impressed by the hand-crafted Moroccan pavilion. His comment, however, was that the Moroccans had obviously spent a great deal of money in building their pavilion.[33] Was it worth it, he asked, when we know that in Morocco there is so much need for other things? They could have built schools or hospitals with the money. And what exactly does this kind of exhibit show if we all know that on the one hand we are saying what a marvellous building they have produced, and on the other we see our police force beating Moroccan beggars in the streets? His comments on South Africa were in a similar vein. While impressed with their display of precious metals, he was most struck by the absence of any reference to the Black population in the exhibition.

Even with regard to Spain itself, enthusiasm for the exhibition did not dull people's ability to see through the displays to another kind of reality.[34] The general opinion seemed to be that Spain, a country that could ill afford it, had spent a lot of money to achieve very little. A year after the event people were talking about the move from optimistic dream to contemporary realities. The Sevillians had made some quick easy money, but now the event was over and the money was gone. Left with high unemployment, inflated prices and a high-speed train that never ran because there were no longer any passengers, this new reality was presented as more enduring, more real.

When I asked people what they had learnt about any foreign nation, and whether these exhibitors had succeeded in their aims to challenge stereotypes, most people replied that they already knew about these countries and what they saw did not challenge that knowledge. There was disappointment with the Japanese exhibit because people had wanted to see the latest technological developments. The decision by the Japanese to present tradition was not reflected upon as the alternative face of Japan. The absence of small technological artefacts was simply noted as a lack, a missed opportunity, which in no way altered people's understandings of Japan as a nation that *could have* displayed intriguing technological innovations.

In fact there was considerable overt reflexivity in the viewing strategies of the visitors with whom I talked. They were aware that their particular contexts of viewing affected what they were prepared to appreciate, even in very basic physical ways. In his discussion of the Czech pavilion one man acknowledged that the reason he had enjoyed it so much was because of the general tensions involved in visiting the Expo site. He had been there for three days, his camera was too heavy, his kidneys had started to hurt, he had had to walk kilometres and kilometres for hours on end every day, he had felt hungry and when he had gone to buy food there was a queue and even when he got to the front of the queue it was only to find that what he wanted had just run out. It did all make him despair a bit. It was in these conditions that he discovered the Czech pavilion. The main impression of the show of light and sound was that it was gentle. He and his friend had sat through from beginning to end with a feeling of great relief. He didn't think it would have been worth queuing for, and other people, presumably with more energy, had come in and out without stopping, confused by the abstract exhibit. This man was aware of the embodied nature of his Expo experience and he was acknowledging that what he learnt was most importantly related to how he felt. Knowledge for him did not simply emerge from an exterior object on which he might gaze. However, it was also explicitly acknowledged that much of what was on show at the Expo had nothing to do with knowledge at all. People recognize artificiality. The biggest attractions tended to be of this kind. The Spanish Moviemax was popular because the seats moved. Why had people queued for up to eight hours to spend a few minutes in a moving seat? The value of this experience was, I suggest, less in the experience itself than in the commodified value of that experience, the fact of having been there, of personal proximity to the renowned. Finally, in terms of this kind of reflexivity, people were well aware that the speed with which they moved around the site prevented anything but a very superficial impression of the exhibits. People didn't remember very clearly what exhibits they had seen in which pavilion. One woman knew that there had been some great dancing in the American Plaza, but she couldn't remember if it was in Santo Domingo, Peru, or one of the others, or was it in fact in the African Plaza! In this sense the speed with which visitors moved around the site probably worked to reinforce stereotypes; it certainly mitigated against the possibility of remembering the details of the visit. Here again we return to the motivations for people's visits, which were primarily to enjoy themselves, not to learn in the sense of gaining new substantive information which they might bring to bear in other areas of their life. Moving seats were simply more interesting than nation states. By visiting the Expo people learnt what a universal exhibition was like, and it was this knowledge which enabled the British couple to whom I referred in Chapter 2, to tell me that the Expo was better than the Welsh Garden Festival but not as good as Disney.

EXPO, DISNEY AND THE WELSH GARDEN FESTIVAL

I have never been to either Disneyland or the Welsh Garden Festival but I am intrigued by the terms of comparison which these British visitors used to express their opinion of the Expo'92. In their comparison they rendered their experiences at these three venues equivalent, and having once invoked such an equivalence, they could then decide which they had enjoyed most, could attribute a rating. Thus, just as we noted how nation states at the Expo were rendered equivalent by the ways in which they were displayed and consumed, so too experiences which could be treated as entirely incommensurable, were in this comparison also brought together for relative evaluation.

However, the differences and similarities between the experiences are not irrelevant; the ways in which they are both brought together and distinguished can tell us things about the practices of consumption inherent in leisure activities. I return to Baudrillard's distinction between representation and simulation and his four successive phases of the image (Baudrillard 1981).

In his interpretation of Disney, Baudrillard does appear to allow that these phases are not in fact consecutive but can be simultaneous, or 'entangled'. However, he also makes the positions incompatible when he claims that what second-order simulations essentially mask are third-order simulations: 'Disneyland is presented as imaginary in order to make us believe that the rest is real, when in fact all of Los Angeles and the America surrounding it are no longer real, but of the order of the hyperreal and of simulation' (Baudrillard 1981: 172).

I would argue that the previous discussion of the consumption of the Expo'92 reveals that such an event can be understood as operating the various phases of the image simultaneously. In the first place visitors do recover basic realities although these may not always be shared. The staging of the event reflected Spain's desire to show itself as a modern and forward-looking European nation, just as it also revealed (to many), that Spain would have trouble in pulling off this public relations exercise. In this sense, if treated as a successful marketing exercise, the Expo could be said to have masked the more basic reality that Spain is a weak European nation whose need to host the Expo demonstrated fragility rather than strength. These possibilities are concurrent if a further message of the Expo is accepted, namely that coherent nation states are themselves imaginary entities and that in this sense the invocation of 'Spain', as social actor, masks the absence of any such basic reality.

Yet the Expo'92 was not equivalent to Disney. Most importantly it was not an event out of time, although it was consumed by many as if it were. It was, as many of these same people noted, a unique event, an event motivated not simply by contemporary international relations, but by the anniversary of another (imaginary) moment, the 'discovery' of the Americas in 1492. Expo exhibitors most definitely played with the production of fantasy worlds, with producing an encapsulated and miniature version of their universe, proposing that cultural difference is no more than consumer choice. Visitors did not expect things to be real at the Expo, but at the same time the exhibits themselves provoked reflection on other realities which were produced as less negotiable. The problem with Baudrillard's analysis of events of this kind is not simply his hyperbolic style, but the fact that such hyperbole masks another basic reality, that people are not simply consumers, or that as consumers they are also simultaneously attending to the world around them in ways that the relations of consumption cannot account for. The implication of this argument is of course that Disney is not equivalent to Baudrillard's depiction of it either. Disney is also in time, once we look at the practices of consumption, the frames of interpretation or concerns which people bring to the event, which their presence embodies and which they carry away with them.

However, experience at the Expo *is* both simulated and commodified and this presents a problem for the way in which experience is integrated into our theories of knowledge. The production model can no longer be assumed to lead to more authentic understandings of human subjectivity. The tendency among anthropologists to favour a notion of cognition tied to embodied action, what Ingold has termed the dwelling perspective,[35] is complicated when we consider that at least some of the knowledge born of immediate experience erases distinctions between the active and the passive, the embodied and the contemplative, the tactile and the visual. In this kind of world it is possible to at least understand Baudrillard's call to action via passivity, the possibility of challenge through silence and the refusal to engage, even if more traditional fields of anthropological enquiry might still predispose us to remain optimistic about the possibilities of recontextualization.

Chapter 6

Conclusion

CULTURAL PROCESS AND CULTURAL FORM

The Expo'92 has provided a contrast between distinctive ways of eliciting the 'cultural'. For the anthropologist interested in practice, an analysis of the exhibition might attend to the processes through which this event was lived, the ways in which the visitors engaged with other persons, objects, technologies, images. And although the focus of attention would be on local interactions, such an analysis would nevertheless concern the global, for the engagement of visitors with the Expo site involved them in relationships which extended far beyond the confines of Seville, as they spent their money, visited the exhibitions and experienced the desire to consume or indeed not to. A focus on the exhibitors could have raised similar issues. Thus, as was shown in Chapters 3 and 4, their cultural practices brought the global into being at the Expo'92. The process of global culture can be found in the ways in which the executives of multinational companies, or the representatives of national governments, envisaged their task and attempted to carry it through, just as it can be found in the ways in which visitors to the Expo site engaged with the exhibition.

An alternative approach to the cultural could involve a characterization of the Expo site as semiotic text or cultural construct. Here interest would be focused on the meanings, intentions, beliefs and values which visitors may or may not recover according to their interest or expertise. Attention in this more hermeneutic approach would be directed to the ways in which meanings are constructed, to the relationships through which particular forms gain significance, or to the beliefs that people hold about the world. In this view, material forms carry meanings which may or may not be brought forth in social interactions but which can nevertheless be analyzed and described as relatively stable co-ordinates in a social field of complex moving relationships.

A focus on process and embodied practice enables a discussion of how people live their lives, how cultural forms emerge and are sustained or replaced in the lived specificity of social relations, how people become who they are. However, the focus on form is an important aspect of the lived worlds not just of the planners, designers and intellectuals but also of all those visitors who engage with these intentions and meanings and are themselves involved in the objectification of experience.[1]

The complementarity of these approaches is not straightforward. There are quite basic incompatibilities between them which prevent a pluralist approach whereby we might seek to simply add a further perspective in the hope of gaining more insight. My argument has been that the two positions involve quite distinct and ultimately incompatible approaches to knowledge, which I have characterized as representational knowledge and knowledge as embodied practice. As argued in Chapter 2, knowledge as representation indicates a process in which a particular state of affairs, the context, is held to be foundational, and at least in this perspective, stable and enduring. In the second case it is the instability and contingency of what is known that is in the foreground. The context is itself emergent, not prior, and understanding of what might momentarily be deemed stable and foundational is achieved via interaction and through attention to social effects.

Many anthropologists seek to distance themselves from the constructionist approach to culture entailed in representational knowledge, arguing that anthropology's contribution to the understanding of social life is to show the ways in which culture is practice, movement, action, life itself. From this perspective there can be no complementarity of approach because the problem with representational knowledge is that it *misrepresents* how people live in the world. The construct metaphor emphasizes a process in which meaning is laid on to reality (Ingold 1993b), requiring specialists to come along and strip the layers away to find out what is really going on. There is a strong implication in the metaphors of construction and deconstruction that there is a more basic reality which might be uncovered in this way, and the constructivists thus promote an implicit primitivism that suggests the existence of a natural or more authentic point of origin before construction began.[2] Others have complained that a focus on the construct has replaced the more complex notion of structure, with its implicit attention to relationships (Gellner 1994: 4).

But the Expo site is tenacious when it comes to constructs, despite the obvious drawbacks to this approach. For a start the exhibition has quite consciously used the effects of the construct to convey particular political messages. Bennett (1988) has shown, for example, the ways in which colonized peoples were used to underlie the rhetoric of progress by serving as its counterpoint. The primitive was deliberately evoked as a point of origin from which the construction of civilized culture could subsequently emerge. Consider again the monastery of Santa Maria de las Cuevas. The building can be symbolically deconstructed, its layers of meaning peeled off like the layers of an onion. But when we get back to the original construction, the origins of this building as a monastery, we find that the origin is of the same order as its subsequent forms, the authentic original is simply another symbolic project, as complex, as human, as social in nature as the building we find today. But the layers are not irrelevant as they constitute the historicity of this material form. Once we have an awareness of them, the nature of these layers becomes integral to our descriptions, whether or not people attend to these interpretative possibilities. After all, what does not happen in social interactions can be as significant as what does. Misunderstandings, omissions and contradictions are the stuff of social life, and a cultural analysis is one which draws attention to possibilities of this kind, one which looks at what is thinkable and the conditions (social relations) that sustain such possibilities. Anthropologists are fascinated by the human facility for making ideas out of other ideas, by the images which make imagination possible, by the cultural consequences of relationships with both human and non-human surroundings (Strathern 1992a). The material constructs of human social life thus demand attention, even in a processual approach to cultural practice.

But the approach has a problem which emerges if we consider the processes through which representational and embodied knowledge are held apart. This brings me back to the status of knowledge and the inevitable move in anthropological practice from process to form, from enactment to representation, from practice to scientific knowledge. In these transformations we find that the attention to embodied specificity is lost in the generation of more general 'social facts'. One of the problems for contemporary anthropology caught in perpetual motion between process and form is the awareness that these (and presumably other) perspectival options do not necessarily amount to knowing more or knowing 'better' because to focus on effect is to efface the preconditions and reconfigure the terms of interaction, while to focus on form abstracts and disembodies the object of analysis, suppresses temporality and leads to partial, even erroneous, representations. We nevertheless have to find ways to establish expertise, and communities of scholars or other 'dependable witnesses' validate facts and distinguish the useful from the worthless. We have returned to the arguments about contextualization and interpretation.

However, there is a more interesting possibility for the interdependence between knowledge as representation and knowledge as effect, if we look at the generation of representational 'knowledge' as embodied practice, if we seek to understand the effects that such objectifications are directed towards.

The practice of the Expo exhibitors shows how attempts to fix certain assumptions as foundational, are, when looked at in terms of effects, about making certain possibilities visible at the expense of others. This was particularly clear in the cases of those intent on producing historical narratives and images of technological and cultural evolution. A focus on the relation between preconditions and outcomes thus raises questions about relative power. The constructed forms of the Expo are the materiality of communicative practice, indeterminate signs dependent on interpretative outcomes, themselves situated within parameters of possibility which are entirely cultural or contingent even when self-evident to the parties concerned, even when tightly confined in apparently over-determined webs of signification.

Knowledge is social practice and a claim to epistemological privilege. For something to be known, there must be a field of expertise or skill through which such knowledge can be formulated or validated. To take an apt example: in 1492 Columbus 'discovered' America, only he did not actually discover it because he did not know he was there. He knew, in fact, that he was off the coast of Japan, following the charts and understandings derived from his study of the voyages of Marco Polo. Before there could be any knowledge of America, the possibilities of its existence had to be established; expert contextualization was required. This contextualization was not possible at the time of Columbus' voyages.[3]

Many Expo visitors set out to enjoy themselves. The claims of those who said that they had not learnt anything, reflect that they were not contextualizing experiences in terms of the particular expertise which would turn experience into knowledge. In this sense my practice differed. Yet, as we have seen in Chapter 5, this formulation begs the question of how we identify and validate experience and expertise. I return to the dilemmas of auto-anthropology. My contextualizing practices were anticipated in many of the exhibits by the producers of the exhibitions who were themselves drawing on the kinds of cultural theory that I was using to contextualize my experiences. The event itself was thoroughly theorized and intellectualized by producers, visitors, journalists, etc. Any anthropological claims to expertise would thus have to invoke further contextualizations, further reflections on the event. Yet this generation of further perspectives was also in some ways pre-empted by the exhibition which tirelessly recontextualized interpretation as choice, consistently undermining expertise by rendering all interpretations equivalent.

This unremitting reflexivity is one of the very distinctive features of contemporary Expos, and one which poses interesting dilemmas for anthropology. As Strathern (1991a) has pointed out, anthropologists are concerned to demonstrate the social and cultural entailments of phenomena, and thus attend among other things to how people draw analogies. Thus at the Expo we could look at the ways in which nation states and multinationals, for example, generated choice, and dynamics of similarity and difference. But the reflexivity of the exhibition also provoked an awareness of analogies between the contextualizing practices of anthropology and of its object of study. An anthropology that attends to effects, that moves away from origins, that no longer attempts to account for the cultural and social preconditions for interactions, is in danger of getting sucked into a kind of deconstructive mimesis, of reproducing the form of that which it is supposedly analysing.[4] As an anthropologist I was seeking to identify the implicit foundational assumptions in the interactions of those I was observing, the patterns and expectations which were activated in their interactions. But in the Expo study, I was also forced to watch myself doing this, as the Expo fascinated visitors by its displays of effects, producing contexts and constructs for visitors to consume, both as representation and as the vehicles for straight sensation. It is only attention to the historicity of the material forms which can prevent this implosion. Anthropological attention to effects is based on theories of cognition that argue for the centrality of embodied interactive processes in the acquisition of knowledge. Advertisers and image brokers who seek to bring effects about, who work to instil desire and to emphasize outcomes as possibilities that consumers can choose without regard for origins, seem to be engaging in similar processes. But anthropology is not calling for an end to origins in quite the same way. By insisting on temporality, on the importance of the history of past relationships, anthropology can emphasize the ways in which preconditions (if not origins) have an implicit presence even if their exact nature or moment is not visibly relevant to present concerns.

Another mirror effect emerges when we consider the problems associated with textual metaphors for cultural processes and the ways in which the construct approach can produce overviews that mitigate against gaps and the unpresentable. One response to such homogenization is to argue for the place of gaps in social and cultural analysis, and by so doing to further the cause of process over that of form. Thus:

> certainty itself appears partial, information intermittent. An answer is another question, a connection a gap, a similarity a difference and vice versa. Wherever we look we are left with the further knowledge that surface understanding conceals gaps and bumps. [... to pay attention to these processes will be to present] an alternative to the usual kinds of claim to be demonstrating intrinsic connections between disparate parts of one's account.
>
> (Strathern 1991a: xxiv)

Again the Expo can demonstrate the effects of such an approach. We find exhibitors questioning the concept of the nation, musing on how to identify culture. It is as if they too are aware of the limits of the cultural construct and are concerned to establish that images are partial and imaginary.

HYBRID INSTITUTIONS

It is in these mirroring effects that the analogies between the exhibition, the nation state and anthropology emerge. If we return to the metaphor of the hybrid it can be seen that one link between these three institutions is that they are all engaged in both the objectification of cultural forms and their simultaneous deconstruction. This practice affects their own identity and they become hybrid institutions in the sense that they seek to promote pure origins, but they also play with the possibilities afforded by their complex, mixed forms. And this should be expected for the hybrid always carries connotations of its own origins. As Latour has shown, hybridization was itself a response to modernist practices of purification and there are no hybrids without natural kinds (Latour 1993).[5]

Another feature of this hybridity is the simultaneity of the modern and the postmodern which the Expo reveals so clearly. Lyotard draws the distinction between modernity and postmodernity in terms of the unpresentable. For him the central modernist question (in terms of art and literature) is how to make visible that there is something which cannot be seen. He distinguishes two strategies:

> (i) the unpresentable [is] put forward only as the missing contents; but the form, because of its recognisable consistency, continues to offer to the reader or viewer matter for solace and pleasure; [and (ii)] the postmodern would be that which, in the modern, puts forward the unpresentable in presentation itself; that which denies itself the solace of good forms, the consensus of a taste which would make it possible to share collectively the nostalgia for the unattainable; that which searches for new presentation, not in order to enjoy them but in order to impart a stronger sense of the unpresentable.
>
> (Lyotard 1984: 149)

In the light of this contrast it is interesting to return to a consideration of the Swiss and Czech pavilions. The Expo used the form of the nation to present the unpresentable. In one way the tactic is modernist; the nation state is unpresentable as a social entity, only a partial image can ever be given, and particular icons are produced to evoke the total entity. However, this representational practice co-exists (even in the same pavilion) with another approach which questions the presentability of the nation state not in terms of a problem of achieving realism, but in terms of the fact that the nation is unpresentable because it is itself an imagined form, an effect not an origin.

Here we can see why anthropology might draw on cultural studies in seeking to describe the ways in which people live mass popular culture. This culture is itself so representational, so reflexive, so imbued with meaning, intention, belief and value, that we cannot afford to ignore the insights of those theorists who write from within this domain. What we cannot expect is that such theories are *generally* applicable as descriptions of lived practice, a point which is particularly visible when they are applied cross-culturally, but which also pertains to western cultural practice.

Baudrillard captures a very important dimension of contemporary social practice in his analysis of the ways in which our lives are embedded in a world of images which are reproduced with increasing ease and frequency thanks to the development and expansion of information technologies.[6] His attention to the relationship between surface and depth, the ubiquity of self-generating, self-mirroring images and the centrality of a notion of experience which has become thoroughly eclectic and superficial, provides a language with which to express aspects of contemporary cultural practice in which the descriptive apparatus of modernist cultural theory is itself implicated and is thus perhaps less able to reveal. However, as ever, an insistence on radical change itself masks continuities, continuities which are more likely to be revealed by attention to the cultural practices of everyday life.

Jameson's famous description of the Bonaventura Hotel emphasizes that the architecture, particularly the concealed or played-down entrances, isolates the hotel's interior from its surroundings, emphasizing the building's aspirations to 'being a total space, a complete world, a kind of miniature city' (Jameson 1984). The Expo was also a miniature city, a total space, a complete world, but its entrances were hardly hidden. In fact the entrances were characterized by architectural excess, and far from producing an isolated, self-contained world, the Expo's central monumental icons, the bridges, marked links to the old city of Seville. The postmodern simulated world seems to claim a place in the territory of Le Corbusier. Expo replaced Seville, providing not just alternative but even simulated versions of other city venues.

Yet it was also a monumental extension of Seville's facilities, and most importantly an instance of its modernization.

Thus, while a particular analysis might illuminate some practices, other kinds of practice are not pre-empted by this first possibility, unless we expect all subjects to be unidimensional and coherent beings. Anthropology's sensitivity to the culturally specific can help to qualify the claims of cultural theorists but more importantly such theoretical claims should be entertained as holding ethnographic status in the study of western cultural process.

And what about the claims concerning the demise of the bourgeois individual subject? While we might want to argue that *in practice* such subjects were never there in the first place, that is at the level of embodied subjectivity, such subjects have had a presence in public institutions (legal, medical, religious, etc.). The individual is a construct – not a fantasy construct of errant social scientists, but a construct produced and acted upon and thus produced as real in practice. Constructs are what public institutions produce (as does all representational practice). Thus anthropology produces constructs despite an interest in process; the nation state produces constructs, although government ministers might be more interested in the effects of multinational capital; the universal exhibition also produces constructs despite contemporary competition for consumers which encourages reflexivity and the generation of sensational effects. What is more, all these instititions watch themselves in the process.

Mitchell's discussion of how exhibitions were instrumental in creating the dualisms through which the modern world is apprehended is an apt observation on the world fairs of the late nineteenth and early twentieth centuries (Mitchell 1988). His work discusses in a particularly illuminating manner how modern ways of representing, interpreting and knowing were used and developed in the European colonial enterprise. This mode of enframing presented the non-modern as disordered, undisciplined, dangerous and unhealthy. Anthropology as a discipline has, despite the narratives of collusion with empire, worked to recover and re-evaluate alternative ways of living in the world. However, in the process, we do of course continue to objectify and employ representational devices. Some might choose to stop writing, others might work to stress that it is important not to reduce the ways in which we know and live in the world to representational forms, and to illustrate the seriousness of this point by giving evidence of alternatives. There is considerable awareness today of the politics of representation, the ways in which such practice is dependent on the separation of self/other, on the imposition of external understandings of order and the exclusions which categorization entails. Our representations are themselves practices/interactions, in which we bring about relations of sameness or sympathy and of antipathy/disagreement. We therefore have to have some responsibility for the ways in which these relations are made to appear and many want to take on this responsibility and engage in the practice of anthropology as critical practice.

This project does not, however, *require* anthropologists to study cultural difference. There is a role for auto-anthropology, and for the critique which the reflexive ethnographic study of our own cultural products can generate. I have tried to show this by revealing that even the universal exhibition is not involved only in representational practices. Expo'92 was, of course, involved in appropriating external realities for the purposes of display and thereby contributing to the sense that the world can be separated from its representation. The exhibits did in many cases work to fix the relationship between the world and its representation and thus establish facts or truths. However, the exhibition simultaneously worked against absolutes and instantiated other ways of knowing. Particularly notable in this regard were the technologies of simulation which operated alongside the technologies of representation.

My argument is not that these technologies fulfilled any liberatory function, for they were shown to be fully inscribed in the commercial activities of transnational companies and the promotional practices of nation states. My interest was rather to make connections which show the ways in which our representational terrain has shifted. The problem for critical anthropology used to concern the ways in which to make our own assumptions visible without setting up others as the opposite of ourselves and producing the kinds of cultural absolutes which we then felt obliged to mediate. Now that culture and context have become self-evident, commodified forms, we are faced with the predicament of how to accommodate the realization that it is not the prerogative of critical cultural theorists to make visible the contingency of representational practice. It therefore seems important to me that critical anthropology should pay some attention to the effect of cultural self-awareness.

To date the argument has been that modern techniques of knowing order the world through representational models that endlessly defer reality. By contrast, non-modern people can dwell in the world with an immediacy that enables them to attend to the effects of social relations, the occurrence and recurrence of practices. There are various possible responses to this scenario. Latour argues that we have never been modern. Alternatively it could be argued that we have never simply been modern even within the confines of key modernist institutions. By considering how representational models work in practice we can produce a more textured self-image through which to work on human practice more generally. And in this enterprise, anthropology and cultural studies could certainly work together to mutual benefit.

Cultural studies offers sophisticated analyses of modern industrial societies and the point has long been taken that it is necessary to look at what people do with texts as well as looking at the social and cultural entailments of the texts themselves. Ethnography, particularly in the domain of audience research, is increasingly used to consider responses to mass-marketed cultural products. It is thus not only the anthropologist who would notice that visitors to the Expo'92 were not simply imploring the spirits of significance to speak. However, the anthropological interest in practical life, in local understandings of the relations of sameness and sympathy between things, in the ways in which analogies are drawn and entities are rendered equivalent, does create a particular space for considering the significance of non-representational practice.

The Expo visitors were not simply after meanings. But then neither were the multinationals simply interested in providing them. The exhibition did give people the world as picture, but there were also many ways in which these distinctions between representation and reality were confounded. There were powerful appeals to the immediacy of sensation, overt attempts to challenge boundaries and to create new hybrid forms. Fujitsu told visitors that the only boundaries were in their minds. Modern temporalities distinguished past, present and future and enabled the narratives of development and progress which informed many of the exhibits – but there were also the moves to establish continuities, to reflect on how we produced these distinctions and at least make space for the imagination of alternatives. As Rabinow notes in relation to the new genetics:

> My argument is simply that these older cultural classifications will be joined by a vast array of new ones, which will cross-cut, partially supersede and eventually redefine the older categories in ways that are well worth monitoring.
>
> (Rabinow 1992: 245)

That radical redefinitions were not forthcoming at the Expo is due to the fact that the interest in innovation was an interest in moving beyond boundaries for commercial ends. The Expo moved visitors into a world of commensurable difference, into the world of the hyper-real, via the presentation of imagined realities which were not aimed at moving us out of our current relationships of consumption but which attempted to change the terms in which we apprehend them, to change the tactics of seduction in an increasingly competitive market. The universal exhibition at the end of the twentieth century acknowledges that reality has been deferred by representational practice and appropriates experience for the realm of representation.

Thus Nicolas Hayek, a senior executive of Swatch (the Swiss Corporation for Microelectronics and Watchmaking), can seek to identify his product with the Swiss cultural environment:

> It is not just the mechanics of the product. It's also the environment around the product. One thing we forget when we analyze global competition is that most products are sold to people who share our culture. Europeans and Americans are the biggest groups in the world buying products from Asia. So if you can surround your product with your own culture – without ever denigrating other cultures or being racist in any way – it can be a powerful advantage.
>
> (quoted in Lury n.d. (1))

Anthropology's traditional concern with cultural difference can contribute a critical sensitivity to statements of this kind. But it can only do so if we are not simultaneously involved in trying to reinstate authentic subjects at the heart of the discipline, discriminating against the validity of the cultural practices of those who read, write and film, and who spend time and energy in enjoying themselves by engaging with the world as picture. It is precisely because the language of critical social science is implicated in the language of cultural commodification that we need to be aware of how analogies are drawn, how similarities and differences are conceptualized, and to do that we need to keep watching.

I have tried to argue that anthropology's particular concern is to notice the ways in which connections are made between disparate cultural and social configurations, to question processes of comparison and distinction, the uses of scale and the place of value. We need to look at how hybrids are made and to what effect, to ask, for example, how it is conceivable that the Expo'92 was not as good as Disney but better than the Welsh Garden Festival.

Notes

1 INTRODUCTION

1 Mitchell (1988: ix).
2 Other international exhibitions are planned but the Expo'92 was to be the last this century with universal status.
3 The Channel Four television production *Visions of Heaven and Hell*, February 1995, provided a most interesting account of this phenomenon.
4 It is not coincidental that the fourth decennial conference of the Association of Social Anthropologists of the Commonwealth was structured around this theme. Under the general rubric of 'The uses of knowledge: global and local relations', the four principal plenary sessions were entitled: (i) Counterwork: managing diverse knowledge; (ii) Religious and cultural certainties (iii) Embodiment and consumption; and (iv) What is social knowledge for?
5 See Miller (1992 and 1994) for an ethnographically based discussion of the ways in which the local is constituted in relation to the global, and thereby also contributes to the construction of global forms.
6 See for example Baudrillard (1979) and Poster (1988).
7 See for example the work of Edwards *et al.* (1993), Edwards (n.d.), Macdonald (1992a, 1992b and 1993a), Macdonald and Silverstone (1990 and 1992), Miller (1992 and 1994) and Silverstone and Hirsch (1982).
8 See Strathern's discussion of the merographic (1991a and 1992d).
9 That debate, fuelled by critiques of theories of knowledge generated by feminism and post-colonialism, will be dealt with in more detail in Chapter 2.
10 See for example Ingold (1993b).
11 The classic example of this genre is Geertz's account of the Balinese cockfight (Geertz 1973), analysed by Crapanzano (1986) and by Clifford (1988).
12 I should stress that my status as journalist went no further than the press accreditation. While I had been commissioned to write a short piece for the *Times Higher Education Supplement* (Harvey 1992), this

was not the primary purpose of my visit. Nor was my purpose to study journalists as a participant observer.

13 See also Macdonald (1993b: 5).

14 I refer here particularly to works such as Clifford (1988), Clifford and Marcus (1986), Mangaro (1987), Marcus and Fisher (1986) and Taussig (1992 and 1993).

15 A comment made by Richard Fardon at a recent conference on context and interpretation held at St Andrews University, Scotland.

16 The relationship between cultural studies and anthropology in the United States has always been somewhat different from that in Britain. In the United States anthropology has traditionally been more concerned with the study of 'culture', while the British school was focused more specifically on social organization. For overview accounts of the development of cultural studies see Gray and McGuigan (1993), Grossberg, Nelson and Treichler (1992), Lave, Duguid, Fernandez and Axel (1992) and Handler (1993).

17 Geertz's article on the Balinese cockfight became a central text for cultural theorists in the 1970s (Geertz 1973).

18 See for example Carlo Ginsburg (1980 and 1990), Patrick Joyce (1995), or the work of cultural historians such as Celia Lury (1993) or Colin Campbell (1987), not to mention the more widely disseminated theorists of cultural history such as Foucault (e.g. 1970) or Benjamin (1970).

19 Writers such as Foucault strongly deny this charge.

20 Ethnography here becomes synonymous with empirical case study, involving more open-ended interactions than survey or formal interview techniques allow. The focus is not however on that specialized meaning of ethnography for anthropologists which entails a focus on the cultural premises implicit in the social interactions in which both researcher and researched are engaged.

21 I am thinking particularly of the relationship between the development of evolutionary theories and their co-option to the eugenics movement. The relationship between anthropology and world fairs was particularly salient in this regard (Rydell 1984). This issue will be dealt with in more detail in Chapter 3.

22 The most cursory review of recent publishers' catalogues generates a plethora of titles in these areas. For example the 1994 catalogue for Leicester University Press has seven new or recent titles on sport, one on the department store and nine on media and communications.

23 See the map on page 145 for further details of which institutions were participating.

24 Further details on this process are given in Chapter 3 as part of a discussion of Spain's motivation for staging this exhibition.

25 This institution was set up in Paris in 1931 to regulate the holding of international exhibitions and to classify their status.

26 A conversation and a coffee with Ben Campbell at the recently renovated Westmorland service station on the M6 motorway in the UK lie behind this comment.

27 Benedict (1983) and Rydell (1993).

28 See Rabinow (1992) and Strathern (1992a).

29 See also Ames (1993: 112).

30 See Macdonald and Silverstone (1992) for a discussion of the problems museums face in renewing information.

31 See Hutnyck (1994) for a detailed treatment of this subject.

2 ANTHROPOLOGY: CAN WE DO ANTHROPOLOGY WHEN CULTURE AND CONTEXT BECOME SELF-EVIDENT?

1 I am grateful to Roy Dilley for his organization of a conference on this topic held in St Andrews in 1994. See Dilley (n.d.). The following section of this chapter follows the argument set out in my contribution to that edited volume.

2 My thanks to Nikos Papastergiadis and Patrick Joyce for their extremely interesting discussion of these points.

3 See for example Clifford and Marcus (1986), Clifford (1988), Fardon (1990), Strathern (1987c and 1991a), Ullin (1991).

4 See for example Foucault (1980a), Stocking (1983), Asad (1986), Clifford (1988), Said (1989).

5 Strathern (1992a) has made the point that the cultural construct is not an exclusively anthropological formulation. It is one that is shared by many cultural analysts and implicitly lies behind the critical project of deconstruction which seeks to denaturalize, reveal and rewrite. The construct renders practices comparable through a process of abstraction in which social entities can be made to stand apart from the relations and lives which produced them.

6 It is important to emphasize that despite claims to the contrary not all cultural studies are written in this vein. There is no reason why the cultural construct should be taken as intrinsically representational in this way, and as Celia Lury has pointed out to me in conversation, cultural theory would benefit from making the distinctions between culture as image, as text, as brand, etc. Lury's work on brand aims precisely to show the ways in which both people and things generate effects, rather than embody meanings (Lury: n.d.(1)).

7 This is an agenda which Sperber has been seeking to establish for anthropology since his publication *On Anthropological Knowledge* (1985), in which he criticizes the general application of the linguistic or communicative model in anthropological analysis. More recently Ingold (1993a) has challenged Sperber's cognitivist approach while maintaining the importance of the study of cognition for contemporary anthropology.

8 James F. Wiener will notice the effects of our conversations here.

9 This theme will be developed with examples in Chapter 3.

10 This theme will be taken up and developed in Chapter 4.

11 For a more detailed discussion on this point see Chapter 3.

12 See Chapters 3 and 4 for more details on this point.

13 See Strathern (1992a) for a parallel discussion of new reproductive technologies.

14 I am grateful to the graduate students of the Anthropology Board, University of California at Santa Cruz for bringing this point up for discussion.

15 In connection with the arguments concerning changes in theoretical approaches outlined in Chapter 1, it is interesting to note that Varela (1992: 330) has argued that it is not a pre-given world, but rather the embodied perceiver that determines how the perceiver can act and be modulated by environmental events. Embodied knowledge cannot be acquired by observation, yet participation at the Expo would not make the embodied knowledge which visitors brought with them accessible either.

16 See Fabian (n.d.) for discussion of a similar distinction between knowledge as representation and knowledge as practice.

17 See Harvey (n.d.) for a fuller development of this argument through a detailed contrast between the Peruvian and the Expo studies.

18 See Macdonald's (1992a, 1992b and 1993a), Macdonald and Silverstone (1990 and 1992) and Bouquet (1993, 1995a, 1995b and 1995c).

3 THE NATION STATE

1 Dumont (1980 and 1986), Handler (1994), Kapferer (1988), Malkki (1990) and Segal and Handler (1992).

2 See Handler (1994) and Kapferer (1988).

3 See Dumont (1980) and Gellner (1983).

4 Foucault's discussions of sexuality and the technology of sex (1980b) are perhaps the most salient examples of his use of this concept of social technologies; one which was developed in the work of de Lauretis on technologies of gender (1987).

5 Foucault (1970).

6 See for example Pickstone (1994) on the development of analytical ways of knowing in the nineteenth century and the ways in which these developments affected the nature of scientific collections and national museums.

7 See Lofgren (1993: 182).

8 See Lofgren (1993) on the ways in which 'typical native scenery' became incorporated as a central element in national cultural heritage.

9 A usage common since the mid-nineteenth century (Oxford English Dictionary).

10 Much recent work in social anthropology on nation states and nationalism is written to challenge the uniformity of this grand transformational narrative. See for example Fox (1990), Handler (1988), Kapferer (1988), Segal (1988), Segal and Handler (1992), Spencer (n.d.) and Verdery (1991a and 1991b).

11 See García Canclini (1995) and Taussig (1993).

12 See Bennett (1988: 129).

13 See for example Hobsbawm (1990), Gellner (1983) and Smith (1986).
14 See for example Smith (1986).
15 See Bennett (1988: 140) for a related discussion on the ways in which universal histories are annexed to national histories at universal exhibitions.
16 See Verdery (1990, 1991a and 1991b).
17 See MacClancy (1993).
18 An extract from the words of welcome offered by King Juan Carlos of Spain Expo'92 (Official Guide: 13).
19 I am grateful to Jeanette Edwards for pointing out that this formulation is to be expected as these are the ways in which we tend to represent the reproductive process to ourselves more generally, and it is precisely the dilemma faced in discussions of the new reproductive technologies in Western Europe.
20 It should be stressed here that 'images' are not understood as representations but operate as experiential or indexical forms in contrast to non-indexical, more encompassing representations. See Hirsch (1995) for a discussion of the interdependence of image and representation in relation to anthropological understandings of landscape.
21 I am arguing this point with particular reference to the Expo'92 as a European event which distinguishes its economic concerns from the other major nexus of exhibitions held in the United States. While these fairs are also intimately concerned with the field of US capitalism, and while the two economic fields are closely inter-related, the nation state as such is less visible as a constitutive entity in the American fairs which have concentrated far more on the relationships between American states.
22 See also Bennett (1988: 143).
23 There were four other pavilions representing international organizations at the Expo'92: the International Olympic Committee; the International Red Cross and Red Crescent Movement; the Inter-American System; the United Nations System.
24 'The European Community in the 1990s', Commission of the European Communities, Brussels (1991) (emphasis added).
25 'The European Community 1992 and beyond', Commission of the European Communities, Luxembourg: Office for Official Publications of the European Communities (1991).
26 Publication of the General Commissariat for Expo'92 Seville: 'The European Community at the Seville World Fair'.
27 There were five of these: Pavilion of the Future, of the Universe, of Navigation, of the Fifteenth Century, of Discovery.
28 The figures quoted here were taken from a television documentary made by 20/20TV for Carlton television and shown in Britain in 1993.
29 It was rather unfortunate that this tree was in fact dead!
30 These comments and those from the following section were made during a lecture to the Manchester Institute of Popular Culture.
31 Gellner (1983) does distinguish three forms of nation state, and Arnason (1990) five, but these typologies do not really correspond to the point that I am making about the specificity of what constitutes

the relationship between ideas of 'nation' and of 'state' in particular times and places.

32 See Williams (1990).

33 The following comments are drawn from a lecture given by Grossberg to the Manchester Institute of Popular Culture and represent one prominent cultural studies approach to issues of culture and globalization.

34 See Ouroussoff (1993) for a fuller discussion of the implications of assuming *a priori* that Western society is lived according to the image and premises of philosophical liberalism.

4 THE UNIVERSAL EXHIBITION: CHANGING RELATIONSHIPS BETWEEN TECHNOLOGY AND CULTURE

1 The other corporate participants were Cruzcampo (Spain's leading brewery), ONCE (Spain's national organization for the blind), and Retevision (a state-funded telecommunications company).

2 See Eco (1983).

3 See also Handler (1990).

4 This connection is made quite explicitly in marketing management studies as Lury discovered:

> Let me give an example of one of these techniques by which the concept of culture as construct is brought into being in the object–people practices of global cosmopolitanism. It concerns the ways in which producers of what have been called tourist-objects seek to control their movement so as to compact user-friendliness into objects, producing their special quality of integrity or trustworthiness. One aspect of this control is the development of the marketing study of product and country images, a specialism which has been described as 'an important subfield of consumer behaviour and marketing management'. Some recent publicity for a book in this field (Papadopoulus and Heslop 1993) claims: 'Thousands of companies use country identifiers as part of their international marketing strategy, and hundreds of researchers have studied the ways these identifiers influence behavior. As markets become more international, the more prominently the origin of products will figure in sellers' and buyers' decisions. The time is ripe for practitioners and academicians to delve into the insights offered in this seminal volume so as to better prepare for meeting the competitive challenges of the global marketplace.' Chapters include: 'Countries as corporate entities in international markets', 'The image of countries as locations for investment', 'Images and events: China before and after Tiananmen Square' and 'Global promotion of country image: do the Olympics count?'.
>
> (Lury n.d.(2))

5 The market visibility that these methods provide is not unambiguously beneficial to the company. I am grateful to John Hutnyk for

pointing out that there is at present a court case in Germany brought by disgruntled Benetton franchisees against the company because of these advertisements.

6 See Breckenridge (1989) on commercial interests in the objectification of the nation.

7 See Lyotard (1984).

8 See Lyotard (1984).

9 I am grateful to Celia Lury for organizing a colloquium at the Centre for Cultural Values, University of Lancaster, where this question was raised.

5 HYBRID SUBJECTS: CITIZENS AS CONSUMERS

1 For a parallel discussion of the immense amount of labour required to produce 'matters of fact' see Shapin and Schaffer (1985).

2 See Jordanova (1989).

3 See for example Bennett (1988), Duncan (1991) and Macdonald (1992b and 1993a).

4 See Duncan (1991: 92) for a discussion of the narratives inherent in museum visits.

5 Bennett notes how at the 1901 Pan-American Exposition visitors were asked to 'Please remember when you get inside the gates you are part of the show' (Bennett 1988: 132).

6 Bennett (1988: 127).

7 Recent anthropological treatments of the subject which themselves provide overviews of how this subject has developed within the field of political economy include Appadurai (1986), Miller (1987) and Silverstone and Hirsch (1992).

8 See for example Jameson (1984 and 1988).

9 See Bourdieu (1984b) on distinction and Benedict (1983) on early world fairs.

10 Machinery was commonly put on display, but such machines were themselves products of mass production.

11 Benjamin (1973: 165).

12 See Lury (n.d.) for an example of new approaches to the analysis of consumer objects.

13 It is also interesting, in the light of discussions in Chapter 4, that many of these sponsors were not US companies at all and included companies from Spain, Belgium, Scotland, England, France, Italy, Germany, Canada, Czechoslovakia and Japan.

14 See Strathern 1992e.

15 See Poster (1988: 7). His reference is to Baudrillard (1983) *In the Shadow of the Silent Majority* (New York: Semiotext(e)).

16 Alpers (1991: 30) makes a similar point about museums, a point which these visitors seemed well aware of: 'museums are perhaps not the best means of offering general education about cultures. It is not only that cultures are not the sum of their materials, but also that books and/or film might do the job much better'.

17 See Macdonald (1993a) for a discussion of the shift towards a visitor-focused relationship between museums and their public in recent years.

18 The dilemmas which this dual brief poses are further exacerbated by a political climate in which museums are expected to operate as entrepreneurial concerns, generating their own income. See Vergo (1989: 2).

19 Greenhalgh (1989: 92–3) notes that the French exhibitions were more festive than their British counterparts, but even the British were concerned to bring together education and diversion in these events. As the Duke of Argyll pronounced at the opening of the Imperial International Exhibition held at the White City in London in 1909, the event provided 'amusement without excess and knowledge without fatigue' (Vergo 1989: 58).

20 See for example Macdonald's discussion of the work of Diane Saunier, who has argued that presenting science as accessible is not the same as actually making it accessible (Macdonald 1992a: 408).

21 See Macdonald (1993a) for discussion of these issues in relation to the British Science Museum.

22 I am referring here in particular to the notion of learning as formal activity as opposed to the understandings of learning in practice as discussed by Lave and Wenger (1991).

23 The inherent pleasure of artificiality is now used quite openly as an advertising strategy, most notably by the company that has recently marketed a butter substitute with a brand name of 'I can't believe it's not butter'.

24 The hosts and hostesses of the British pavilion were referred to as navigators.

25 Heelas (1994) discusses a similar commodification of religious experience.

26 See Foucault (1970) and Crary (1990).

27 Note Heidegger's observation that 'The world picture does not change from an earlier medieval one into a modern one, but rather the fact that the world becomes picture at all is what distinguishes the essence of the modern age' (Heidegger 1977: 130).

28 See Crary (1990).

29 Note Schaffer's fascinating account of the role of self-experiment in the work of Boas and Rivers (Schaffer 1994). Also Poole's discussion of the photography of Hiram Bingham whose primary concern was to chronicle not the content of the view but his attainment of that view (Poole 1995).

30 From Paul Virilio (1989: 20).

31 See for example Lave and Wenger (1991).

32 See Hutnyck (1994: 125) for a fascinating discussion of the ways in which tourists construct experiences through the medium of preservable two-dimensional representations.

33 The declared cost of this pavilion was US $35 million.

34 Alternative realities would, of course, also be mediated by images.

The point is simply that such contrasts affect how and what people know.

35 Ingold (1993b: 152).

6 CONCLUSION

1 These objectifications are not necessarily immobile and omnipresent as Ingold has argued; the video diary of such a visit is an example of mobile and partial representation. The significance of the mobility of video images was discussed in Chapter 5.

2 See the introduction to Harvey and Gow (1994) for a discussion of this point in relation to the literature on gender.

3 See O'Gorman (1961).

4 I would argue that this is a hazard for all analyses of mass popular culture. See Jameson (1984) on the auto-referentiality of all modern culture which turns upon itself and designates its own cultural production as its content.

5 For further discussion on the concept of the hybrid see García Canclini (1995).

6 Featherstone (1991) has also expressed similar ideas about consumer culture.

Bibliography

Alpers, S. (1991) 'The museum as a way of seeing', in I. Karp and S. Lavine (eds) *Exhibiting Cultures: the Poetics and Politics of Museum Display*, Washington: Smithsonian Institution Press, 25–32.

Ames, M. (1992) *Cannibal Tours and Glass Boxes: the Anthropology of Museums*, Vancouver: University of British Columbia Press.

Anderson, B. (1983) *Imagined Communities: Reflections on the Origins and Spread of Nationalism*, London: Verso.

Ang, I. (1992) 'Living-room wars: new technologies, audience measurement and the tactics of television consumption', in R. Silverstone and E. Hirsch (eds) *Consuming Technologies: Media and Information in Domestic Spaces*, London: Routledge, 131–45.

Appadurai, A. (ed.) (1986) *The Social Life of Things: Commodities in Cultural Perspective*, Cambridge: Cambridge University Press.

Arnason, J. (1990) 'Nationalism, globalization and modernity', *Theory, Culture and Society*, 7: 207–36.

Asad, T. (1986) 'The concept of cultural translation in British social anthropology', in J. Clifford and G. Marcus (eds) *Writing Culture*, Berkeley: University of California Press, 146–64.

Baudrillard, J. (1968) 'The system of objects', reprinted and translated in M. Poster (ed.) (1988) *Jean Baudrillard: Selected Writings*, Cambridge: Cambridge University Press, 10–28.

—— (1979) 'On seduction', reprinted and translated in M. Poster (ed.) (1988) *Jean Baudrillard: Selected Writings*, Cambridge: Cambridge University Press, 149–65.

—— (1981) 'Simulacra and simulations', reprinted in M. Poster (ed.) (1988) *Jean Baudrillard: Selected Writings*, Cambridge: Cambridge University Press, 166–84.

—— (1993) 'The evil demon of images and the precession of simulacra', in T. Docherty (ed.) *Postmodernism: a Reader*, London: Harvester Wheatsheaf, 194–9.

Benedict, B. (1983) *The Anthropology of World's Fairs: San Francisco's Panama Pacific International Exposition of 1915*, London: Scolar Press.

Benjamin, W. (1970) *Illuminations*, London: Fontana.

—— (1973) *Charles Baudelaire: a Lyric Poet in the Era of High Capitalism*, London: New Left Books.

—— (1978) *Reflections*, New York: Harcourt, Brace, Jovanovich.

Bennett, T. (1988) 'The exhibitionary complex', in N. Dirks, G. Eley and S. Ortner (eds) (1994) *Culture/Power/History: a Reader in Contemporary Social Theory*, Princeton: Princeton University Press, 123–54.

Bhabha, H. (1985) 'Signs taken for wonders: questions of ambivalence and authority under a tree outside Delhi, May 1817', *Critical Inquiry* 12(1): 144–65.

Boon, J. (1982) *Other Tribes, Other Scribes*, Ithaca, N.Y.: Cornell University Press.

Bouquet, M. (1993) *Man-ape Ape-man. Pithecanthropus in het Pesthuis, Leiden*, Leiden: Nationaal Natuurhistorisch Museum (exhibition catalogue).

—— (1995a) 'Exhibiting *homo erectus* in 1993', in R. Corbey and B. Theunissen (eds) *Ape, Man, Apeman: Changing Views since 1600*, Leiden: Department of Prehistory, Leiden University.

—— (1995b) 'Exhibiting knowledge: the trees of Dubois, Haeckel, Jesse and Rivers at the Pithecanthropus Centennial Exhibition', in M. Strathern (ed.) *Shifting Contexts*, London: Routledge.

—— (1995c) 'Strangers in paradise', *Science as Culture* 5 1(22): 3–56.

Bourdieu, P. (1977) 'The economics of linguistic exchange', *Social Science Information* SVI(6): 645–68.

—— (1984a) *Homo Academicus*, Oxford: Polity Press.

—— (1984b) *Distinction*, London: Routledge.

Breckenridge, C. (1989) 'The aesthetics and politics of colonial collecting: India at world fairs', *Comparative Studies in Society and History* 31(2): 195–236.

Brooker, P. (1992) *Modernism/Postmodernism*, London: Longman.

Buck-Morss, S. (1991) *The Dialectics of Seeing: Walter Benjamin and the Arcades Project*, Cambridge, Mass.: MIT Press.

Campbell, C. (1987) *The Romantic Ethic and the Spirit of Modern Consumerism*, Oxford: Blackwell.

Clifford, J. (1988) *The Predicament of Culture: Twentieth Century Ethnography, Literature and Art*, Cambridge, Mass.: Harvard University Press.

—— (1992) 'Traveling cultures', in L. Grossberg, C. Nelson and P. Treichler (eds) *Cultural Studies*, London: Routledge, 96–116.

Clifford, J. and Marcus, G. (eds) (1986) *Writing Culture*, Berkeley: University of California Press.

Coombes, A. (1991) 'Ethnography and the formation of national and cultural identities' in S. Hiller (ed.) *The Myth of Primitivism: Perspectives on Art*, London: Routledge, 189–214.

Crapanzano, V. (1986) 'Hermes' dilemma: the masking of subversion in ethnographic description', in J. Clifford and G. Marcus (eds) *Writing Culture*, Berkeley: University of California Press, 51–76.

Crary, J. (1990) *Techniques of the Observer. On Vision and Modernity in the Nineteenth Century*, Cambridge, Mass.: MIT Press.

Crary, J. and Kwinter S. (eds) (1993) *Incorporations*, New York: Zone Books.

Crimp, D. (1993) 'The photographic activity of postmodernism', in T. Docherty (ed.) *Postmodernism: a Reader*, London: Harvester Wheatsheaf, 172–9.

de Certeau, M. (1984) *The Practice of Everyday Life*, Berkeley: University of California Press.

de Lauretis, T. (1987) *Technologies of Gender: Essays on Theory, Film and Fiction*, Bloomington: Indiana University Press.

Deleuze, G. (1983/1986) *Cinema I: The Movement – Image*, Minneapolis: University of Minnesota Press.

Deleuze, G. and Guattari, F. (1972/1977) *Anti-Oedipus: Capitalism and Schizophrenia*, Vol. I translated by R. Hurley, M. Seem and H. Lane, New York: Viking.

Department of Trade and Industry (DTI) (1992) 'Britain at Expo'92: information sheet'.

Dilley, R. (n.d.) *Context and Interpretation*, Oxford: Oxford University Press.

Docherty, T. (ed.) (1993) *Postmodernism: a Reader*, London: Harvester Wheatsheaf.

Dumont, L. (1980) *Homo Hierarchicus: the Caste System and its Implications*, Chicago: University of Chicago Press.

—— (1986) *Essays on Individualism*, Chicago: University of Chicago Press.

Duncan, C. (1991) 'Art museums and the ritual of citizenship', in I. Karp and S. Lavine (eds) *Exhibiting Cultures: the Poetics and Politics of Museum Display*, Washington: Smithsonian Institution Press, 88–103.

Eco, U. (1983) *Travels in Hyper Reality*, San Diego, California: Harcourt, Brace, Jovanovich.

Edwards, J., Franklin, S., Hirsch, E., Price, F. and Strathern, M. (1993) *Technologies of Procreation: Kinship in the Age of Assisted Conception*, Manchester: Manchester University Press.

Edwards, J. (n.d.) 'Born and bred: idioms of relatedness in late twentieth-century England' (manuscript).

Expo (1992a) *Expo'92 Official Guide*, Seville: Sociedad Estatal para la Exposicion Universal Sevilla 92, S.A.

—— (1992b) Expo Press Dossier.

—— (1992) *The Best of the Expo*, Seville: On Site Publications.

Fabian, J. (n.d.) 'Ethnographic misunderstanding and the perils of context', in R. Dilley (ed.) *Context and Interpretation*, Oxford: Oxford University Press (forthcoming).

Fardon, R. (ed.) (1990) *Localizing Strategies: Regional Traditions of Ethnographic Writing*, Edinburgh: Academic Press.

Featherstone, M. (1991) *Consumer Culture and Postmodernism*, London: Sage.

Foster, H. (ed.) (1983) *Discussions in Contemporary Culture*, Seattle: Bay Press.

—— (1983) *Postmodern Culture*, Seattle: Bay Press.

Foucault, M. (1970) *The Order of Things: an Archaeology of the Human Sciences*, London: Tavistock.

—— (1980a) *Power/Knowledge: Selected Interviews and Other Writings 1972–77*, ed. C. Gordon, Brighton: Harvester.

—— (1980b) *The History of Sexuality*, Vol. 1: *An Introduction*, translated Robert Hurley, New York: Vintage Books.

Fox, R. (ed.) (1990) *Nationalist Ideologies and the Production of National Cultures*, American Ethnological Society Monograph Series, No. 2.

Friedman, J. (1994) *Cultural Identity and Global Process*, London: Sage.

García Canclini, N. (1995) 'Rethinking identity in times of globalization', (with postscript by P. Harvey), in N. Papastergiadis (ed.) *Art and Design*, special issue on 'Art and cultural difference: hybrids and clusters', 36–43.

Geertz, C. (1973) 'Deep play: notes on a Balinese cockfight', in C. Geertz *The Interpretation of Culture*, New York: Basic Books.

Gell, A. (1986) 'Newcomers to the world of goods: consumption among the Muria Gonds', in A. Appadurai (ed.) *The Social Life of Things: Commodities in Cultural Perspective*, Cambridge: Cambridge University Press, 110–38.

Gellner, E. (1983) *Nations and Nationalism*, Oxford: Blackwell.

—— (1994) 'What do we need now? Social anthropology and its new global context', *The Times Literary Supplement*, 16 July: 3–4.

Ginsburg, C. (1980) *The Cheese and the Worms: the Cosmos of a Sixteenth Century Miller*, Baltimore: The Johns Hopkins University Press.

—— (1990) 'The inquisitor as anthropologist', in C. Ginsburg *Myths, Emblems, Clues*, London: Hutchinson Radius, 158–64.

Gray, A. and McGuigan, J. (eds) (1993) *Studying Culture: an Introductory Reader*, London: Edward Arnold.

Greenhalgh, P. (1991) 'Education, entertainment and politics: lessons from the great international exhibitions', in P. Vergo (ed.) *The New Museology*, London: Reaktion Books, 74–98.

Grimshaw, A. and Hart, K. (1993) *Anthropology and the Crisis of the Intellectuals*, Cambridge: Prickly Pear Press.

Grossberg, L., Nelson, C. and Treichler, P. (eds) (1992) *Cultural Studies*, London: Routledge.

Guattari, F. (1992) 'Regimes, pathways, subjects', in J. Crary and S. Kwinter (eds) *Incorporations*, New York: Zone Books, 16–37.

Gupta, A. and Ferguson, J. (1992) 'Beyond "Culture": space, identity and the politics of difference', *Cultural Anthropology* 7(1): 6–23.

Handler, R. (1988) *Quebecois Nationalism and the Politics of Culture*, Madison: University of Wisconsin Press.

—— (1990) 'Consuming culture (genuine and spurious) as style', *Cultural Anthropology* 5(3): 346–57.

—— (1993) 'Anthropology is dead! Long live anthropology!', *American Anthropologist* 95(4): 991–9.

—— (1994) 'Is "identity" a useful cross-cultural concept?', in J. Gillis (ed.) *Commemorations: the Politics of National identity*, Princeton: Princeton University Press.

Hannerz, U. (1993) 'The withering away of the nation?', *Ethnos* 3–4: 377–91.

Haraway, D. (1989) *Primate Visions: Gender, Race and Nature in the World of Modern Science*, London: Routledge.

—— (1991) *Simians, Cyborgs and Women: the Reinvention of Nature*, New York: Chapman and Hall.

—— (n.d.) 'Modest Witness @ Second Millenium. The FemaleMan© Meets OncoMouse™' (manuscript).

Harvey, D. (1989) *The Condition of Postmodernity*, Oxford: Blackwell.

Harvey, P. (1992) 'A joke across the ocean blue', *The Times Higher Education Supplement*, 6 November: 15.

—— (n.d.) 'Culture and context: the effects of visibility', in R. Dilley (ed.) *Context and Interpretation*, Oxford: Oxford University Press.

Harvey, P. and Gow, P. (eds) (1994) *Sex and Violence: Issues in Experience and Representation*, London: Routledge.

Heelas, P. (1994) 'The limits of consumption and the post-modern "religion" of the New Age', in R. Keat, N. Whiteley and N. Abercrombie (eds) *The Authority of the Consumer*, London: Routledge, 102–15.

Heidegger, M. (1977) 'The age of the world picture', in *The Question Concerning Technology and Other Essays*, translated W. Lovitt, New York: Harper and Row.

Herzfeld, M. (1987) *Anthropology Through the Looking Glass: Critical Ethnography in the Margins of Europe*, Cambridge: Cambridge University Press.

Hirsch, E. (1995) 'Landscape: between place and space', in E. Hirsch and M. O'Hanlon (eds) *The Anthropology of Landscape: Perspectives on Place and Space*, Oxford: Clarendon Press, 1–30.

Hobsbawm, E. (1990) *Nations and Nationalism since 1780. Programme, Myth, Reality*, Cambridge: Cambridge University Press.

Hobsbawm, E. and Ranger, T. (1983) *The Invention of Tradition*, Cambridge: Cambridge University Press.

Hutnyk, J. (1994) 'The rumour of Calcutta: tourism, charity and the apparatus of representation', Ph.D. thesis, University of Melbourne.

Ingold, T. (1990) 'The concept of society is theoretically obsolete', Group for Debates in Anthropological Theory, No. 1.

—— (1992) Editorial in *Man* 27: 693–6.

—— (1993a) 'Technology, language, intelligence: a reconsideration of basic concepts', in K. Gibson and T. Ingold (eds) *Tools, Language and Cognition in Human Evolution*, Cambridge: Cambridge University Press, 449–72.

—— (1993b) 'The temporality of the landscape', *World Archaeology* 25(2): 152–74.

Jameson, F. (1984) 'Postmodernism, or the cultural logic of late capitalism', *New Left Review* 146: 53–92.

—— (1988) 'Postmodernism and consumer society', in E. A. Kaplan (ed.) *Postmodernism and its Discontents*, London: Verso, 13–29.

Jordanova, L. (1989) 'Objects of knowledge: a historical perspective on museums', in P. Vergo (ed.) *The New Museology*, London: Reaktion Books, 22–40.

Joyce, P. (1995) 'The end of social history?', in *Social History* 20(1): 73–91.

Kapferer, B. (1988) *Legends of People, Myths of State: Violence, Intolerance, and Political Culture in Sri Lanka and Australia*, Washington: Smithsonian Institution Press.

Karp, I. and Levine, S. (1991) *Exhibiting Cultures: the Poetics and Politics of Museum Display*, Washington: Smithsonian Institution Press.

Latour, B. (1993) *We Have Never Been Modern*, translated C. Porter, Cambridge, Mass.: Harvard University Press.

Lave, J., Duguid, P., Fernandez, N. and Axel, E. (1992) 'Coming of age in Birmingham: cultural studies and conceptions of subjectivity', in *Annual Review of Anthropology* 21: 257–82.

Lave, J. and Wenger, E. (1991) *Situated Learning: Legitimate Peripheral Participation*, New York: Cambridge University Press.

Lofgren, O. (1993) 'Materializing the nation in Sweden and America', *Ethnos* 3–4: 161–96.

Lury, C. (1993) *Cultural Rights: Technology, Legality and Personality*, London: Routledge.

—— (n.d. (1)) 'The united colours of diversity: Benetton, branding and cultural essentialism' (unpublished article).

—— (n.d. (2)) 'The objects of travel' (unpublished article).

Lyotard, J.-F. (1984) *The Postmodern Condition: a Report on Knowledge*, translated by G. Bennington and B. Massumi, Manchester: Manchester University Press, reprinted in P. Brooker (ed.) *Modernism/Postmodernism*, London: Longman, 139–50.

MacClancy, J. (1993) 'At play with identity in the Basque Arena', in S. Macdonald (ed.) *Inside European Identities: Ethnography in Western Europe*, Oxford: Berg, 84–98.

McDonald, M. (1993) 'The construction of difference: an anthropological approach to stereotypes', in S. Macdonald (ed.) *Inside European Identities: Ethnography in Western Europe*, Oxford: Berg, 219–36.

Macdonald, S. (1992a) 'Cultural imagining among museum visitors: a case study', *Museum Management and Curatorship* 11: 401–9.

—— (1992b) 'Reconfigurations of knowledge in science museums', unpublished manuscript.

—— (1993a) 'Un nouveau "corps de visiteurs"? Musées et changements culturels', *Publics et Musées* 3: 13–27.

—— (1993b) 'Identity complexes in Western Europe: social anthropological perspectives', in S. Macdonald (ed.) *Inside European Identities: Ethnography in Western Europe*, Oxford: Berg, 1–26.

Macdonald, S. and Silverstone, R. (1990) 'Rewriting the museums' fictions: taxonomies, stories and readers', *Cultural Studies* 4: 2.

—— (1992) 'Science on display: the representation of scientific controversy in museum exhibitions', *Public Understanding of Science* 1: 68–87.

McRobbie, A. (1992) 'Post-Marxism and cultural studies: a postscript', in L. Grossberg, C. Nelson and P. Treichler (eds) *Cultural Studies*, London: Routledge, 719–30.

Malkki, L. (1990) 'Context and consciousness: local conditions for the production of historical and national thought among Hutu refugees in Tanzania', in R. Fox (ed.) *Nationalist Ideologies and the Production of National Cultures*, American Ethnological Society Monograph Series, No. 2, 32–62.

Mangaro, M. (ed.) (1990) *Modernist Anthropology: from Fieldwork to Text*, Princeton: Princeton University Press.

Marcus, G. and Fisher, M. (1986) *Anthropology as Cultural Critique*, Chicago: University of Chicago Press.

Miller, D. (1987) *Material Culture and Mass Consumption*, Oxford: Blackwell.

—— (1992) 'The young and the restless in Trinidad: a case of the local and the global in mass consumption', in R. Silverstone and E. Hirsch (eds) *Consuming Technologies: Media and Information in Domestic Spaces*, London: Routledge, 163–82.

—— (1994) *Modernity – An Ethnographic Approach: Dualism and Mass Consumption in Trinidad*, Oxford: Berg.

Mitchell, T. (1988) *Colonizing Egypt*, Cambridge: Cambridge University Press.

O'Gorman, E. (1961) *The Invention of America: an Inquiry into the Historical Nature of the New World and the Meaning of its History*, Bloomington: University of Louisiana Press.

Ouroussoff, A. (1993) 'Illusions of rationality: false premises of the liberal tradition', *Man* 28(2): 281–98.

Papadopoulus, N. and Heslop, L. A. (1993) *Product-Country Images: Impact and Role in International Marketing*, New York: Haworth Press.

Pearson, R. (1994) *European Nationalism 1789–1920*, London: Longman.

Pickstone, J. (1994) 'Museological science: the place of the analytical/comparative in nineteenth-century science, technology and medicine', *History of Science*, xxxii: 111–38.

Poole, D. (1996) *Vision, Race, and Modernity: a Visual Economy of the Andean Image World*, Princeton: Princeton University Press.

Poster, M. (ed.) (1988) *Jean Baudrillard: Selected Writings*, Cambridge: Polity Press.

Rabinow, P. (1989) *French Modern: Norms and Forms of the Social Environment*, London: MIT Press.

—— (1992) 'Artificiality and enlightenment: from sociobiology to biosociality', in J. Crary and S. Kwinter (eds) *Incorporations*, New York: Zone Books, 234–52.

Robertson, R. (1992) *Globalization: Social Theory and Global Culture*, London: Sage.

Rydell, R. (1984) *All the World's a Fair: Visions of Empire at American International Expositions, 1976–1916*, Chicago: University of Chicago Press.

—— (1993) *World of Fairs: the Century-of-Progress Expositions*, Chicago: University of Chicago Press.

Said, E. (1978) *Orientalism*, New York: Pantheon.

—— (1989) 'Representing the colonized: anthropology's interlocutors', *Critical Inquiry* 15(2): 205–25.

—— (1993) *Culture and Imperialism*, London: Chatto and Windus.

Saunier, D. (1988) 'Museology and scientific culture', *Impact of Science on Society* 38:4, 337–53.

Schaffer, S. (1994) *From Physics to Anthropology – And Back Again*, Cambridge: Prickly Pear Press.

Schwartz, H. (1992) 'Torque: the new kinaesthetic of the twentieth century', in J. Crary and S. Kwinter (eds) *Incorporations*, New York: Zone Books, 70–126.

Sears, J. (1989) *Sacred Places: American Tourist Attractions in the Nineteenth Century*, Oxford: Oxford University Press.

Segal, D. A. (1988) 'Nationalism, comparatively speaking', *Journal of Historical Sociology* 1(3): 301–21.

Segal, D. A. and Handler, R. (1992) 'How European is nationalism?' *Social Analysis* 32: 1–15.

Shapin, S. and Schaffer, S. (1985) *Leviathan and the Air-Pump: Hobbes, Boyle and the Experimental Life*, Princeton: Princeton University Press.

Silverstone, R. and Hirsch, E. (eds) (1992) *Consuming Technologies: Media and Information in Domestic Spaces*, London: Routledge.

Smith, A. (1986) *The Ethnic Origins of Nations*, Oxford: Blackwell.

Spencer, J. (n.d.) 'Bringing it all back home: nationalism, education and modernity in Sri Lanka', (manuscript).

Sperber, D. (1985) *On Anthropological Knowledge*, Cambridge: Cambridge University Press.

Stewart, S. (1993) *On Longing: Narratives of the Miniature, the Gigantic, the Souvenir, the Collection*, London: Duke University Press.

Stocking, G. (ed.) (1983) *Observers Observed: Essays on Ethnographic Fieldwork*, Madison: University of Wisconsin Press.

Stolcke, V. 'Talking culture: new boundaries, new rhetorics of exclusion in Europe', *Current Anthropology*, 36: 1–24.

Strathern, M. (1987a) 'The limits of auto-anthropology', in A. Jackson (ed.) *Anthropology at Home*, London: Tavistock Publications, 16–37.

—— (1987b) 'An awkward relationship: the case of feminism and anthropology', *Signs* 12(2): 276–92.

—— (1987c) 'Out of context: the persuasive fictions of anthropology', *Current Anthropology* 28(3): 251–81.

—— (1988) *The Gender of the Gift. Problems with Women and Problems with Society in Melanesia*, Berkeley and Los Angeles: University of California Press.

—— (1991a) *Partial Connections*, Lanham, Md.: Rowman and Littlefield Publishers Inc.

—— (1991b) 'Introduction', in M. Godelier and M. Strathern (eds) *Big Men and Great Men: Personifications of Power in Melanesia*, Cambridge: Cambridge University Press.

—— (1992a) *Reproducing the Future: Essays on Anthropology, Kinship and the New Reproductive Technologies*, Manchester: Manchester University Press.

—— (1992b) 'The uses of knowledge: global and local relations', open letter to participants at the ASA IV Decennial Conference, held in Oxford, July 1993.

—— (1992c) 'The decomposition of an event', *Cultural Anthropology* 7(2): 244–54.

—— (1992d) *After Nature: English Kinship in the Late Twentieth Century*, Cambridge: Cambridge University Press.

—— (1992e) 'Foreword: the mirror of technology', in R. Silverstone and E. Hirsch (eds) (1992) *Consuming Technologies: Media and Information in Domestic Spaces*, London: Routledge, vii-xiii.

—— (1995) *Shifting Contexts*, Vol. 1 of ASA IV Decennial Conference Series: 'The uses of knowledge: global and local relations', London: Routledge.

Taussig, M. (1992) *The Nervous System*, London: Routledge.

—— (1993) *Mimesis and Alterity*, London: Routledge.

Ullin, R. (1991) 'Critical anthropology twenty years later: modernism and postmodernism in anthropology', *Critique of Anthropology* II(1): 63–89.

Varela, F. (1992) 'The reenchantment of the concrete', in J. Crary and S. Kwinter (eds) *Incorporations*, New York: Zone Books, 320–38.

Verdery, K. (1990) 'The production and defense of "the Romanian Nation" 1900 to World War II', in R. Fox (ed.) *Nationalist Ideologies and the Production of National Cultures*, American Ethnological Society Monograph Series, No. 2, 81–111.

—— (1991a) 'Theorizing socialism: a prologue to the "transition" ', *American Ethnologist* 18: 419–39.

—— (1991b) *National Ideology under Socialism: Identity and Cultural Politics in Ceausescu's Romania*, Berkeley: University of California Press.

Vergo, P. (ed.) (1989) *The New Museology*, London: Reaktion Books.

—— (1989) 'The reticent object', in P. Vergo (ed.) *The New Museology*, London: Reaktion Books, 41–59.

Virilio, P. (1989) *War and Cinema: the Logistics of Perception*, translated P. Camiller, London: Verso.

Wagner, R. (1975) *The Invention of Culture*, Englewood Cliffs, New Jersey: Prentice-Hall.

—— (1991) 'The fractal person', in M. Godelier and M. Strathern (eds) *Big Men and Great Men: Personifications of Power in Melanesia*, Cambridge: Cambridge University Press.

Williams, B. (1990) 'Nationalism, traditionalism and the problem of cultural inauthenticity', in R. Fox (ed.) (1990) *Nationalist Ideologies and the Production of National Cultures*, American Ethnological Society Monograph Series, No. 2, 112–29.

Young, R. (1995) *Colonial Desire: Hybridity in Theory, Culture and Race*, London: Routledge.

Index

Note: Illustrations are indicated by italic print.